Write to the Point

WRITE TO THE POINT

The Byoir Style Book
for Press Material

by JOHN STAHR

Introduction by L. L. L. Golden

THE MACMILLAN COMPANY
COLLIER-MACMILLAN LTD., LONDON

FIRST PRINTING

The Macmillan Company
Collier-Macmillan Canada Ltd., Toronto, Ontario
Printed in the United States of America

TO *Frank G. Stahr*

AND *Gerry Swinehart*

Contents

Introduction

Gerald Frederick Swinehart, who died on October 31, 1966, was perceptive as well as practical. As the co-founder in 1930 with Carl Byoir of the public relations firm Carl Byoir & Associates, he knew that working with print media was basic. He also knew that the kind of material his firm distributed would largely determine its acceptability. As a former newspaperman he had seen the sloppy copy that came in to the city desk and was appalled by the lack of professionalism in the stream of press releases every newspaper receives.

Gerry Swinehart, through his long career, constantly sought and fought for good clean copy. When he first crossed the street in 1926 to become director of advertising and publicity for the cities of Palm Beach and West Palm Beach he decided that all copy distributed from his shop would be written in good style and clearly understandable, so it would gain the respect of the newsmen who flipped the pages of his releases.

In the mid-30s, when the Byoir agency was beginning to grow in New York, Swinehart began to see the fulfillment of his long-time goal of having "a hard-bitten city editor riding herd on our copy."

Then in 1944 Swinehart decided to formalize his quest for flawless copy by the creation of a style book for his staff writers. He hoped this would not only assure uniformity and greater clarity in writing but would set standards for his staff, the kind of standards that would be acceptable to the best newsmen.

But that in itself was not enough for Gerry Swinehart. A style book without a central clearing desk to assure quality control of copy would not be effective. So a central desk was set up to assure that the staff writers would follow style, that there would be a continuing check on adherence to style. The man chosen to compile the style book and see that it was followed was John Stahr, with Byoir since 1935.

There was a "full-cycle" or "second-generation" aspect to this, for the seeds of Swinehart's respect for straightforward, proper copy had been planted by his first city editor, Frank G. Stahr (John's father), on the Elkhart (Indiana) *Truth*. As it happened, Gerry and John had gone to work on that paper the same week, in 1922, for Frank G., to whom Gerry often referred as "the best small-town city editor I ever knew." In the intervening years John had been for four years sports editor of the South Bend *Tribune* and, for another four, a writer and editor with the AP Feature Service.

This volume is the result of twenty-four years of careful checking of all copy moving out of the Byoir offices. Style books have changed, in a few particulars, as usage has changed, and this one has grown larger, through the years, with the addition of a good deal of illustrative material, plucked from the copy stream. The organization of the internal-use style book has been altered in *Write to the Point,* and in many cases there has been a shift of emphasis.

For anyone who has worked on the desk of a newspaper and has seen what has come in over the transom, there is hope that this volume will be read. Not that there is anything startlingly original in *Write to the Point.* It's an old story, but there are some new twists in the way some of its points are made. It is because this volume fills a need for those—and there are far too many—who have failed to master the fundamentals of effective writing that this first publication for use outside the Byoir firm is so welcome.

Effective communication is difficult enough without the complications caused by failure to follow the rules of grammar and writing style. John Stahr's work should be valuable to all who write and edit for press and internal purposes.

L. L. L. GOLDEN

Write to the Point

I.

Small
Editorial

An alert reader could get the impression that this book is committed to what grammar teachers used to call (maybe they still do) the "narrow constructionist" viewpoint.

He could point to its unwillingness to let "comprise" be used as though synonymous with "compose"; to acquiesce in the use of "literally" as a mere emphasizer; to look tolerantly upon applying "dilemma" to any sort of problem or difficulty whatever; to consent to using "infer" as a synonym for "imply."

"Why don't you let the language grow—let it be a living language?" is the usual reproach of those who take the liberal line in such matters.

By all means, let us let it grow . . . let us be hospitable to imaginative, effective new uses, new combinations, coinages, and "graduations" from slang, the vernacular or technical jargon to acceptability and currency.

But there is a difference between letting words grow and live, on the one hand, and letting them decay, on the other. The view here is that allowing words such as the examples above to be given broader meanings—in some cases meanings that are opposite to their original, etymologically recognizable meanings—tends to dilute, devitalize and devalue the words, or at least contribute to their delinquency, when they really have genuine values and identities that deserve preserving.

This is not to say that each and any such loose use is a semantic sin, but people who take pride in their writing should at least be mindful of the erosion that is furthered by indulging in such slipshoddities.

II.

Three
Rights
to
Remember

This book is designed to be useful in a relatively painless way to anyone who needs to put words on paper for any reason. It is an outgrowth of a booklet created many years ago as a style guide for a public relations firm.

The theory behind that original idea was that public relations written material has a special need for meeting the highest standards of copy quality, because editors have an instinctive resistance to any material offered to them by an outside source. That resistance is by no means as strong these days as it used to be, but it is still an important and often decisive factor.

And if any kind of message is ever going to reach the public upon whose "relations" it is expected to have an effect, the first hurdle that it has to clear en route to making that ultimate impression is the critical, not to say skeptical, scrutiny of the editor or news director to whom it is offered.

All publications have definite style standards, embracing a great many rather universally accepted policies as to punctuation, capitalization and structure. And of course they all believe firmly in good spelling and proper syntax. It was reasoned that copy that could be immediately recognized by an editor as reflecting skill and care in its preparation and format would have a much better chance of getting a sympathetic reading than copy that in any way betrayed an unfamiliarity with the way things are done in the best editorial circles.

The late Gerry Swinehart* wrote:

In the years since 1944 [date of the first edition] the writing business—especially in the realm of daily journalism—has shaken itself loose from many deep-rooted habits. Professional practitioners of plain speaking and writing have analyzed and psychoanalyzed the copy of many newspapers and the output of the two biggest press associations.

Most people agree that the net result has been more zip, more readability, more naturalness, less triteness, less stodginess, in today's papers. We should, at the very least, keep pace with the progress being made elsewhere. Perhaps you feel that putting emphasis on standardization of style is the very opposite of what we should do if we want to encourage progressive and free-swinging journalese.

The answer to that is two-fold. One part is this: The attractiveness of present-day informality in newspaper writing is not achieved by abandoning standards of uniformity, typographic consistency and good taste. These are eternal verities in this business. Not even the plainest-speaking apostle of plainwriting has dared suggest that we forget all our punctuation and capitalization standards and enter an era of lexicographic laissez-faire.

The other part of the answer is that this manual is not intended as a strait jacket for your words. Beyond setting forth our general style standards it seeks to encourage lively, uninhibited writing.

* See Introduction.

This book reflects many of the typographic and other lessons all
of us have absorbed through many years of laboring in the
journalistic and public relations vineyards.
Our code is that even the most colorful and entertaining writing
can have consistency, logic, and meticulous perfection of
form, without losing its color, its originality, or its attractiveness.

Through the years, and through three subsequent editions of
that in-house style book, much evidence has come to light of
its usefulness to others. Industrial executives of client companies
have requested extra copies for the use of their secretaries. . . .
Byoir employee wives and brothers-in-law who are teachers of
English in high school or junior high have testified that in some
respects they've found it more effective—more fun, too—than
their official grammar textbooks. . . . Church and Chamber of
Commerce secretaries have said it's a help in the preparation of
bulletins. . . . A number of newspapers have used it to supple-
ment their own style dicta, and it is in use in a number of college
journalism and public relations courses.

Possibly the chief reasons many persons besides professional
writers and editors found an ancestor of this book helpful was
that it made its syntactical points with real-life examples, rather
than by citing grammar rules.

So the book has a kinship with boarding-house hash. Remember? "You don't make it; it accumulates!" Much of this book just
accumulated.

It is almost traditional of publication style books to disclaim
any intent to "teach people how to write." That's true of this
one, also. But more than a few fellows who were already pretty
fair hands as newspaper writers have commented that many of
the little "lessons" now embodied in the book's examples have
contributed to their appreciation of various fine points of making
oneself understood on paper.

Since the subtitle of this book is *The Byoir Style Book for Press Material* you might well be tempted to wonder if there is a "Byoir style." Well, if you're thinking in terms of anything like a Steinbeck style, a Picasso style, or a Mozart style, the answer is of course no. A style book's main purpose is to ensure physical uniformity and consistency, not to set guidelines designed to produce any particular artistic flavor.

Still, it may be useful to anyone who needs to put words on paper to mention a few of the broad style parameters—now *there's* a good, scientific-sounding fad word for you!—whose application may be assumed to have had some effect on the characteristics of Byoir output.

Some years ago we collaborated with Eugene A. Murphy, editor of *Instrumentation*, a publication of Honeywell's industrial division, on a small booklet of helpful hints for the company's technical writers. The chief reason for doing it was to make the point that writing on technical subjects could be more effective if it did not cleave so tightly to the use of "engineeringese"— the roundabout, overqualified, slightly pompous language some engineers tend to use when putting things in writing.

Why Not Just TELL Them? was the title. It not only capsulized the point of that booklet but has been found useful many times, in scores of writing situations—from big stories to little memos. Indeed, it's practically "our policy" at Byoir.

Now, if that phrase is an effective capsule aid for remembering how to approach the *writing* of something, here is a formula we have found effective for many years in the *editing* of copy.

Actually, it's a paraphrase of an old razor-blade commercial. You'll recognize the rhythm: *Copy has to*

Look Right   Sound Right   Be Right

Few things "look wronger" to an editor than a misspelled word. They may be small, but to him they're ugly. If you aren't naturally a good speller, you can still ensure against such fluffs by using the dictionary—diligently. Which dictionary? Well, it doesn't really make that much difference. The main thing is to be willing to stop and look. It's not a bad idea to get acquainted with several different ones. They agree pretty well on most things, anyway.

Going even beyond this, it is important not to offer material that, although it carefully avoids making an actual misleading statement itself, invites a rewrite man to draw an erroneous conclusion in the course of his striving for, perhaps, a simpler sentence.

Somebody Cares

Apparently even in this permissive age there still are a lot of people around who care about writing things right. And saying them right. They have not abandoned the belief that there is some usefulness, as well as virtue, in constructing sentences in which the various paired elements agree in number, gender and tense. Many even go so far as to insist that it's still a good idea to know and heed the difference between the subjective and objective cases and the effect they have on pronouns in the English (or even the American) language.

Presumably you are among those who care.

On all sides we hear and read, in this final third of the twentieth century, doleful comments about the apparent decline of interest on the part of the current younger generation in clear and grammatical writing or speaking. Certainly the complaints about spelling are widespread and anguished.

If there is this general decline, one often-advanced theory is that it is largely caused by today's dominance of electronics in communication.

There are two prongs to this spear: One is that, because people rely so heavily on non-word-reading impressions from radio, television and movies for what they know about the world—even its history, geography and politics, and by all means its religions and sports—they get less and less practice at reading. The other is that, in the very area of listening where the impressions are most insistently and repetitiously (and perhaps habit-formingly) made, the standards of grammar are being deliberately, patronizingly and demagogically degraded.

An obviously well-groomed and intelligent boy of about 11 is required in a television commercial to say, "Dad, can you drive as *good* as this bus driver?" because a gaggle of ad copy writers, in their wisdom, decided this somehow would have more impact on the audience than the same thought expressed in correct grammar. And you probably cannot even remember the last time you heard the subjective pronoun "we" used in a commercial, because it has become almost an article of faith with commercial copy writers that us common people would think them commercials was getting too highbrow if the elegant young lady with the black eye was to say, "*We* smokers would rather..."

Coffee commercial, after She puts in five cups' worth of grounds:

HE: "Hey, who's going to drink all that coffee?"

SHE: "Me." ("*I* am" would be just as emphatic and by no means pedantic.)

Bread commercial. Two 7-year-olds—not ragamuffins, respectable kids.

HE: "I'm gonna eat all 18 slices" (of this bread).

SHE: "Aren't [sic] you gonna put nothin' on it?"

A newscaster, with a completely straight face, signs off a midday show with: "Herbert and *me* wish you a good afternoon." . . . In a kitchen scene, one housewife exclaims: "This is just what you need—a cleanser that *don't* fool around!" The soft-drink salesman says, "If you wanta give a party, or just *lay* around in a hammock, be sure to have _____ on hand." And so on, hour after hour.

There is obviously a temptation to feel that in these days, when one can learn almost all he needs to know just by looking at and listening to capsulizations of almost everything, it is not terribly important to be able to write accurately and persuasively, because nobody's reading.

What Does It Say—Exactly?

We who do hold to the older-fashioned view about the written word can find plenty of consolation. Think how often we hear a head of state or even a mayor or a lower official say that he will not be ready to comment on a given accusation or proposition "until I have had a chance to study the text" (or whatever).

Parents not infrequently face the problem of having to figure out exactly what the schoolteacher or the principal means in a note sent home about Junior. New words, many of them softeners, are coming in. A parent has to keep up with such undulations in the language if he's going to know what the teacher meant in saying that "in the previous semester Willie was among our underachievers, probably because he was overcompensating."

And if those who've grown accustomed to making their living by putting words on paper are fearful that the electronics age is sounding a death knell to that art (well, craft, then), perhaps they can be comforted a bit by the thought that even the best of speeches and commentaries that come into our consciousness via the ear have been "put on paper" first.

For a couple of years there had been rumblings of how "the computers" might soon be taking over even such a creative function as preparing a news release. The idea was generally pooh-poohed, but even so there was a ripple of nervous-relief-type laughter in public relations and ad agency offices when, in a test, a computer was asked to translate the phrase *"out of sight, out of mind"*—and came out with *"invisible* idiot."

A copy chief is frequently asked by staff writers for suggestions on how to become a more effective writer. One answer is this: You can make yourself a more imaginative writer by being constantly analytical, critical and appreciative *while reading.*

Every time you read a news or feature lead that seems to you
to be good, so the advice goes, pause a moment and ask yourself if, given the same situation, you would have had the wit to
choose that approach, and those words. Maybe you wouldn't,
but the very act of your thinking about it, and appreciating the
fact that the man who did the story came up with an approach
that was effective, can sharpen you and may increase your own
chances of coming up with a provocative lead the next time.

The same technique can be applied, in reverse, each time you
find yourself reading a story that seems less than satisfying for
one reason or another. A sure symptom is your having to reread
a paragraph to understand it. Try to decide what there is about
it that lets your mind drift or get off on the wrong track. Think
how *you* would have written it better.

The affirmative side of this "reader appreciation" technique
can be used also in the form of "listener appreciation." Many
of the reports delivered by radio and TV newscasters show evidence of extremely tight writing, and a writer can find himself
appreciating the skill with which just a couple of paragraphs
have been put together. Listen especially to the windup paragraph of an Eric Sevareid commentary, and notice with what
flawless grammar, impeccable sentence structure and rhetorical
precision he wraps up his closing observation.

What does all this have to do with a style book? Well, it
is true that a dictionary definition of "stylebook" (all one word)
is: "a book containing rules of usage in typography, punctuation, etc., employed by printers, editors and writers." But this
little volume is deliberately identified as a style book (two
words), and "style" has enough variety of meanings to justify
our going a mite beyond the mere mechanics of punctuation
and typography.

For one thing, the writing of public relations material has a higher *fight-for-his-attention* quotient than
almost any other kind of writing. That's because this
is material that's to be offered free to some editor who

has, at his elbow, literally reams of other eligible material, much of it from internal sources that have a much stronger claim on his attention.

That's the primary reason why p.r. material should be as tight and as "quick" as it can be made. Visualize a busy editor (is there any other kind?) confronted with more material than he needs. He wants to get through that stack as fast as possible. He is strongly tempted to brush off into the wastebasket any item as soon as he spots anything in it that causes him to say to himself, "Oh, baloney!"

So it's a fight—a fight to keep him from deciding that your story is too long for the news it contains; that it is badly constructed and therefore would require somebody's time to rearrange it; that it is too self-serving; that it tries too hard to assure credit for the client at the expense of reporting its news from the kind of viewpoint the publication has.

Since every paragraph is a fight, we shouldn't start any paragraph with anything less than the quickest, most logical and most attention-grabbing way of saying the next thing that should be said.

A big consideration in this "fight" plan is, in a sense, typographic. An editor is understandably dismayed when he picks

up a "release" and sees that it runs on for two full pages or more of solid double-spaced typed text.

Give him a break, figuratively and literally. How? By the use of subheads, an occasional indented paragraph, or, when the material justifies it, tabular matter.

Subheads especially can do a lot to help convince an editor that maybe there *is* something for his publication in this story, after all—because you can slip in a provocative one-liner here and there, often bringing to the editor's notice something interesting that wasn't compelling enough to have been worked into the first three or four paragraphs.

One thing that often comes up in any discussion of style, from either the literary or the typographic standpoint, is the matter of length of paragraphs and length of sentences. Look to Thomas Wolfe and William Faulkner for the long ones, and to any of quite a few newspapers for the short ones.

The shop where the material for this book evolved has long said, when asked about broad, sweeping "always do thises" and "never do thats" in our writing, that "the only absolute must we have along that line is that we absolutely have no absolute musts."

This means that around here nobody's making a syllables-per-sentence count or a words-per-sentence or a sentences-per-paragraph one (although anyone is free to make such mathematical analyses of his own output if he wishes to do so). Perhaps it's the *Why Not Just TELL Them?* formula at work.

Short sentences undoubtedly are desirable. They're easy to understand. They can be useful as a mental punctuation tactic in a text that otherwise, of necessity, is running to fairly long ones. But short sentences are not necessarily better than long ones, in every context.

Look at Winston Churchill. Or listen to him on recordings. No one ever accused him of being hard to understand, did they? He paid his readers and listeners the supreme compliment of assuming that they would be able to follow him through many a sentence that was very long indeed; and they did follow him, didn't they? Not only through sentences, but through blood, toil, tears and sweat.

Of course, almost none of us has the skill, either in our written rhetoric or in our vocal inflections, to lead readers or listeners through long thoughts as unerringly as did Sir Winston. But we can try. We can dare to use a long sentence where it's fitting, and to use a very short one likewise.

In consulting later sections that refer to matters of punctuation, capitalization, spelling, headlines, release lines and the like, the reader should be aware that these reflect Carl Byoir & Associates preferences and are not offered as absolute and invariable standards to be "thrust upon" everyone.

Also, while the book approaches all matters primarily from the standpoint of public relations output, the hope is that its guidelines may be found useful to almost anyone who has the responsibility for making any kind of document *Look Right, Sound Right* and *Be Right*.

A DIFFICULT DECISION was faced by the copy desk just a few paragraphs before the end of this section: whether to perpetuate the popular version ("blood, sweat and tears") of the famous Churchill promise or to quote him correctly and cause a majority of readers to assume the book had booted one. Unless both Bartlett's and Oxford have it wrong, "blood, toil, tears and sweat" was what he said.

III.

Analyze, Organize, Visualize

People in the public relations business have to do a lot of writing beyond that involved in publicity releases and captions.

Letters (short and long), memos (also short and long), speech texts, instructional or viewpoint-promulgating pamphlets, and resolutions—all these are embodied in the p.r. man's workaday writing obligations. But such chores are by no means the exclusive concern of public relations people. People in all walks of life get involved in them, and almost anyone can profit by developing his skill and effectiveness in putting together such communications.

In the preceding section there was mention of the "why not just tell them?" approach and its possible usefulness in helping anyone draw a bead on a news or feature story.

There is no intention here to imply that all writing can be reduced to a guaranteed-results formula. Yet it can be argued that in the kind of writing most people do—people other than real-live fiction-writing authors—some guidelines that go beyond the standard ones of mere grammatical rectitude may be useful. Such guides can help one attain such desirable attributes as logical approach, smooth flow, clarity, conviction and all-around effectiveness.

One of these, one that may have somewhat more applicability to letters, memos, speeches, resolutions and special material than it does to releases, is the reminder to "analyze, organize and visualize." It is of course true that most sensible writers do these three things—perhaps subconsciously—but the theory here is that it does no harm for him to be reminded to do them *consciously*. So:

ANALYZE. Take a keen look—as objective as you can—at the whole subject with which you wish to deal (or have to). Decide what's good about it, what's bad about it; what's interesting about it, what's dull about it; what's its central fact, what's its tributary facts; what you want the reader—or listener—to conclude from what you say about it.

ORGANIZE. Make a few scratch pad notes. Noodle it a bit. Make an outline, if it's that long a piece. And, in the case of a speech, make an outline even if it's quite short. Decide what you're going to say *first*, then how the *second* and *third* and *subsequent* things hook on.

VISUALIZE your audience, either of readers or listeners. Do your best to put yourself in their shoes. . . . If you were there, what would grab your attention, what would keep your attention, what would make the kind of permanent impression on you that you, the writer or speaker, want to make?

Letters

There are any number of sources from which one can get guidance as to correct *format* for business letters, with examples of the form of salutations, spacing, complimentary closings, forms of address to dignitaries and so forth. Indeed, several dictionaries have extremely complete sections on this. As Casey Stengel would say, you can look it up.

For several decades there has been a considerable tendency, especially among persons involved with any area of the communications business but by no means confined to them, to get away from time-honored formal salutations and polite but possibly meaningless sign-offs.

Many persons have succumbed so utterly to "Dear John-ophobia" that they flatly refuse to "Dear" anybody when they start a letter. This probably should be regarded as a rather extreme position, because most of the world is not yet ready to relinquish the right to be "Deared" in that particular context.

But certainly in informal letters—even business ones among persons who are not strangers—there is opportunity for "starting off" in a way that contributes more to acceptance of the message you are sending than will the routine "Dear Soandso."

Some persons who devote a little extra mental effort to this problem have applied the **visualize** ideal. That is, such a writer visualizes himself walking into Soandso's office or approaching him on the train-station platform or at a cocktail party with a particular bit of news or view or question—and then he starts off the letter in *just about* the same way he would start the conversation. (Of course, it is not feasible to try to convert into printed words the exact language one would use in conversation, but just going through this process of visualizing the parallel can give your letter a lift.)

Another tip on letter writing, applicable to either business or personal letters, is: Try to remember always to start right off referring to the *recipient's* person or interest rather than to *you,* the *writer.* Ironically, a great many amateur writers of solicitation letters pursue this theory, wittingly or un-, in the buttery opening phrase but then commit this syntactical sin: "Dear Mr. Gottrox: As one of Bingville's most influential citizens, *I* would like to call to your attention . . ."

It has been conservatively estimated that at least 33 per cent of all such letters fall into this kind of *appositional non sequitur* in some way or other.

In letters, be alert to opportunities for relieving the monotony of a long parade of solid paragraphs. If your letter has something worth saying, chances are there is a particular paragraph that deserves—and would benefit by—being *indented*. Another way of both relieving and capturing the eye of your letter reader is by *tabulating* key points of argument or entreaty or mere conditions. It makes it easier for him to give you a point-by-point reply, too. Seize opportunities to use the a, b, c or 1, 2, 3 structuring—but be careful not to overdo it.

Keeping even the "regular" paragraphs short always helps, too.

Memos

All the above apply also to communications cast in the form of memos, whether intraoffice, interoffice or international. Incidentally, one school of thought favors putting letters into the form of memos instead of regular letter form. The theory is that this solves the problem for those who (1) find themselves getting self-conscious about this "Dear Soandso" business and/or (2) feel intensely hypocritical about closing with "Sincerely yours" a letter in which they realize they have been more polite than sincere in a few spots.

One type of memo, quite popular in the public relations business, is known as the background memo. And a first cousin of this is the fact sheet. It is good to remember that when you label a document a fact sheet you should make sure not only that everything you put in it is a fact (not an opinion) but also that the structure and language hew strictly to the line of presenting facts *in factual form,* as stark and lean as possible. Do not indulge in any romantic word-painting.

Speeches

Anyone who goes to church or Kiwanis or Rotary or anywhere that speeches are made will recognize, upon reflection, that it's a lot easier to stay awake if the sermon or speech has been truly **organized**—and especially if the speaker keeps making it apparent that the speech does have structure and organization. That's the reason for the strong recommendation that an *outline* be made for a speech.

That outline should be more than just a check list of things to be said. It should start with the reason(s) for making such a speech, anyway, proceed through a readily recognizable pattern of X points of Information or Persuasion—each identified in its appropriate relationship to the Objective Sought—and conclude with a clear indication of what the speaker wants or expects his audience to do or think or feel, if anything. (And if there *isn't* "anything" he shouldn't be making the speech.)

Organizing a speech into X points not only helps the speaker and the audience to understand what he's "drivin' at," but also helps the audience to have some idea of how much more of this there's going to be. What is more discouraging than listening to a speaker go on for quite some time and then hearing him draw a deep breath and say: "Now, in the *second* place—"? Especially when he hasn't told you how many points, all told, he intends to make.

Resolutions

WHEREAS there is no distinction or literary grace whatever in the thrice-thrice-familiar "Whereas" form of resolution, let us hereby resolve to *find some other way.* The "whereas" structure not only puts a great strain on one's semicolon and comma expertise but rigidly limits—because of the stream-of-consciousness sentence structure—the ability to say what you want to say.

There are other ways of doing it. Holding off the actual reference to "resolving" until the final sentence, you can call your document a memorandum of appreciation or commendation or gratitude or whatever, or a statement of policy or intent, or some other. Remembering that what was good enough for Thomas Jefferson and his fellow forefathers ought to be good enough for us, we might even make bold to call our document a Declaration.

Come to think of it, how do you think that great document of July 4, 1776 would sound with a "Whereas," hobbling every paragraph?

A final note, reprising the **organize** idea with respect to news and feature stories:

Most of the best reporters have the knack, either by instinct or gained through conscious cultivation, of keeping themselves reminded that the reader *does not know* all the writer knows about the subject of the story. It is important to remember this. It helps the writer take stock, after each sentence or at least each paragraph, and say to himself: "Now what will the reader want to know, on the basis of what he has found out thus far?" And the best reporters then proceed to answer that unuttered question. And the reader gets a quiet, happy feeling of satisfaction.

IV.

Ripples
in the
Copy
Stream

"A true critick," observed Joseph Addison in *The Spectator*, "ought to dwell rather upon excellencies than imperfections" (in the process of discovering the concealed beauties of a writer).

That nobly affirmative viewpoint is not going to be challenged here. It should apply with equal validity to the thought processes of any true editor or pedagogue seeking to find and point out pathways of writing rectitude.

But, human nature being what it is and the facts of editorial life being what they are, there simply are nowhere near as many "excellencies" to dwell upon in the daily grist as there are imperfections. And, with all due respect to the value of the affirmative approach, it has to be recognized that there is more news in sin than in righteousness, anyway. In any walk of life a lesson learned from doing something (or seeing something done) the wrong way has sharper impact than a mere reminder that something was done right.

So in the following collection of examples, actually fished from copy streams, the examples of how not to do it will easily outnumber the instances of conspicuous excellence.

Participants in copy seminars often ask what are the two or

three "most aggravating" or "most recurrent" imperfections encountered in present-day written matter of the kind produced for journalistic outlets (aside, that is, from mere misspellings and such basic grammar goofs as failing to make subjects and predicates agree in number and tense).

The desk out of whose experience this book has grown has a "triple-A" answer:

Attribution   Affectations   Arithmetic

Two of these, attribution and arithmetic, are to some degree more likely to be problems in public relations copy than in other writing. That's because: (1) attribution is particularly necessary in matter offered any news outlet from any outside source; and (2) there is widespread unfamiliarity among "writing folk" with the true arithmetic significance of "more" "over" and "greater" when used in combination with a percentage increase or a "times" increase—and yet it is especially important that publicity material be scrupulously accurate in such reporting.

"Affectations" is a broad term for purposes of this discussion. It covers (see subdivisions in the Ripples) the "Passé Participles," "Misfiring Metaphors," "Non Sequiturs," "Watch Your Figure(s)" and other aberrations, so many of which result from a writer's affecting what he assumes to be a journalistic or literary way of slinging his words.

But lest this introduction take on stronger overtones of scolding and impatience than are intended, perhaps we should just move on to the Ripples and let them speak for themselves.

Attribution

ATTRIBUTION, either *direct* or *implied*, is one of the constant requirements of publicity material. Failure to "attribute" mentions of the quality, ability, longevity, desirability or any of a thousand other "ities" of an instrument, a product or even a situation quickly stamps a release as having been written by someone who has not kept himself reminded of the care with which newspapers themselves treat *any subjective* expression.

Sometimes insertion of just a word or two can make a favorable reference to some item *palatable* to the editor scanning copy with traditionally skeptical eye—words like "designed to," "reported" or "described as." These are a few of the most faithful and useful servants in this role. Of course they are not direct attribution, but in many an instance a fairly sweeping statement about what some new device *can do*, a statement that would cause any alert editor to cry out in skepticism and exasperation, "*Who says* it can?" can be smoothed out by the adroit insertion of such a phrase, so that the editor's neck veins will not bulge.

A less frequent quasi attribution, but quick and painless, especially in somewhat technical descriptions, is "rated." For instance, you might want to say that a certain new process is 10 to 15 times as sensitive as conventional techniques used in the industry, and you don't want to clutter up this sentence with still another "officials said." So you just write: "It is *rated* 10 to 15 times . . ." This greatly eases the curse of the *flat statement,* and does it quickly, without overloading the sentence. (Incidentally, the question of whether the claim is *true* or not has no bearing on *the way* it should be said. It's just that the papers do not make flat statements on such matters. Read 'em—watchfully— and see.) "Geared to" is another phrase useful here.

AN ATTRIBUTE of an ATTRIBUTION, desirably, is that it occurs at an appropriate point, not at an unnecessary one. If you are writing about a new warehouse and say it will provide faster handling, make possible most efficient inventory control, etc., or give *any* subjective descriptions, that's where you need attribution. Then, if you are bored at putting in all those "he saids" or "the announcement saids," you can justifiably leave out the attribution when you come to mention that it will be a one-story building 80 by 200 feet. . . . Conversely, here's an attribution that was stuck in at a particularly inappropriate spot: "One kitchen convenience that is appreciated during hot weather is the automatic ice-maker in the refrigerator. According to Alfred Fridge, president of the association, it is located in the freezing compartment of the refrigerator."

Often you may have a release that is a strict matter-of-fact announcement, with no subjective element at all in the opening statement, yet you have the requirement of crediting an official for making it. Many times it is possible, in such a case, to let the first sentence stand as a flat statement, without tacking on any "it was announced by" phrase. But then you should promptly work the name of the official into the second paragraph, preferably by having him say something that in some way interprets or explains the move.

INCOMPLETE ATTRIBUTION—From a wired dispatch from Hot Springs, Ark.:

American involvement in what he called "an indigenous Asian civil war" is unjust, Sen. Fulbright said, and more Senate members are coming around to this point of view.

QUESTION: Who made the observation that "more Senate members are coming around to this point of view"—Sen. Fulbright or the anonymous filer of the dispatch? Almost surely it was a view expressed by the senator, but the sentence structure fails to make that clear.

Affectations

Misfiring Metaphors

An indignant editorialist writing about the Berlin Wall: "It has been most successful in frustrating the Western powers, who had *stood supinely by* while this abomination was reared under their

noses." This is an even neater trick than that of those persons who
are constantly swooning and lying there prone on their back.

ADDLED ADAGE: "Barnum's observation that 'there's one born
every minute' is especially true in the home-buying market where
many young hopefuls are *shorn* daily because they trusted, etc."
Ringing in a folksy saying like this can do more harm than
good if you let the metaphor misfire, either out of thoughtless-
ness or ignorance. Barnum was talking about *suckers,* not *lambs.*
So, *hooked* was the word, if you must have a figurative one.

THE ENGINE THAT WALKS LIKE A BEAR: "These figures (on steel
production) should warn America that the Soviet economy is hitting *on all fours* in turning out basic supplies . . ."

LUCKY PANDORA? It is always a good idea to know something
of what lies behind a figurative word or phrase. Otherwise we
run the risk of using one that is ironically or hilariously inappropriate (or of misspelling it, as in the oft-seen "bell weather").
For example, we would *not* write that "A pair of pillowcases
turned out to be a Pandora's Box for an Oklahoma City housewife" (it brought her a bonanza of cigarette-premium gifts).
Preserving the figurative approach, we might make it: "A pair
of pillowcases turned out to be stuffed with a lot more than
feathers for an Oklahoma City housewife."

A bunch of the boys were discussing the turndown of the
President's airline strike settlement proposal by the machinist's
union, and one observed, "Boy, ol' LBJ has sure got a hot po-
tato by the ears now!"

PICTURESQUE words and phrases are fine, when deftly and
thinkingly employed. But one should be sure the word is perti-
nent as well as picturesque. A recent obit of a celebrated admiral
contained the sentence: "In one instance Admiral Jones brought
in a whole convoy of supply ships to the beaches near Savo

Island without losing a single one, despite attacks by an umbrella of Japanese planes." Umbrella is the figurative word there, but it is 180 degrees out of phase. In air-warfare parlance umbrella (quite logically) refers to *defensive* measures *shielding* something below.

WORDY—"This pair of computers is being used to control the information explosion that is engulfing the medical sciences." (1) Mixed metaphor: an explosion does not engulf; (2) fad word: haven't we had about enough figurative *explosions?* (3) the computers couldn't possibly control such a phenomenon. . . . They could help cope with it.

HARDLY PERENNIAL—"The Suchandsuch business, like Topsy, grows and grows and grows."

This is one of the classic examples of the misfiring of a figure of speech when the user of it either doesn't know, or forgets, what made this word or phrase notable, or at least remarkable, in the first place. Topsy did *not* grow and grow and grow; she never did get to be a very sizable girl. Her comment, "I 'spect I growed," was in answer to a question about who her parents were or where she was born. She 'lowed as how nobody borned her, she jest growed. . . . So let's give Topsy a long-deserved vacation from being a symbol of sudden or prodigious growth. If you're tired (or scared) of mushrooms, there's always Jack's beanstalk available for a pole vault over the literary garden wall; or you might like to try the Biblical "like a cedar in Lebanon" (so grows a righteous man—tall as well as straight).

Watch Your Figure(s)

ALL-TIME CHAMPION instance of the unhappy result of using familiar figures of speech without being familiar with the original allusion: "She should be like Caesar's wife—all things to all men"!

"This makes a delicious dish, the kind of food that youngsters regard as manna from the gods."

Manna is not associated with special deliciousness but with the providential nature of its source (upper-case Heaven, not "the gods"). The stuff that the gods regarded as mighty tasty was ambrosia.

". . . costs have continued to rise, but this brand still proudly refuses to *knuckle down* to increasing economic pressure, and holds the price line." It is true that dictionaries indicate that "knuckle down" has a secondary meaning of "to yield, give in" (synonymous with "knuckle *under*"), but its first definition—and the one that comes readily to mind of most people—is almost the opposite, namely: "to work energetically, apply oneself seriously" (from getting one's knuckles down at the taw line in marbles so as to make a good, legal shot).

BIBLE STUDY—"The fisherman turned litterbug is a spoilsport. If these litterers don't mend their ways, all nimrods will suffer through loss of favorite fishing grounds."

Sounds okay, but it isn't. Nimrod was, in the Bible (Genesis), a mighty hunter. Ergo, today, nimrods are hunters, not fishers. Don't let that rod spoil you. It's not a fishing rod.

A HEAD FOR FIGURES of speech is helpful if you're going to make use of figurative language. NOTE:

"Rails *Hamstrung*, Official Tells Kiwanis Club" was the head over a story that led off with the comment that government regulation was "dislocating the *backbone* of American transportation."

Awareness of anatomy helps, too!

"Publicity cannot do much if it's dealing merely with a new package, new additive or any other creative *crutch harnessed* to *replate* the old *façade*."

crutch—helps a human being walk
harnessed—what happens to horses

replate—rejuvenate the silver, or make over a page on the
newspaper

façade—front of a building

Passé Participles

Probably the No. 1 affectation in the realm of daily journalism
is the use of the deferred-subject style of sentences. To wit:

"A 'natural' fertilizer, he predicted that it would solve many
problems," etc., etc.

"GLAMORIZED by writers of South Sea tales from Joseph Conrad
to Robert Louis Stevenson, copra has become the No. 3 import
of the Port of San Francisco."

When you arrange those thoughts in that deferred-subject
sequence you distinctly imply that there is a cause-and-effect
hookup between copra's having been glamorized by the writers
and its current economic importance. But there isn't any such
relationship, and the writer did not mean to imply it. He should
have said simply: "Copra—a commodity that has figured in many
a romantic South Sea tale but is unfamiliar to most Americans—
has become the No. 3 import of the Port of San Francisco."

"Never touched by human hands throughout the 10 separate
manufacturing operations required to produce them, Stanley re-
searchers now have succeeded in . . ."

"Completed three years ago, the plant is 301 feet by 339 feet
and is a one-story structure containing . . ." (A plant of exactly
that size could have been completed 50 years ago, or yesterday.)

"A Harvard graduate, he was formerly national affairs editor
of *The Reporter* magazine."

Back in the days when there was a political wisecrack that the
best way to get appointed to the Supreme Court was to "go to

Harvard and turn left" a sentence like the above might, if written with the intent of conveying a wry hint of cause-and-effect, make sense.

"Brown, a man of thinning hair, is held in Cell No. 10 at the St. Louis County jail."
Because that's the one with the padded ceiling?

Not everybody has a clear understanding of what a dangling participle is. Until a worse (hence, better) example comes along —which may be never—here's one that should make it pretty clear:
"By transferring these duties to an experienced factor enables management to turn time and energy to more productive channels."

"Stored in an air-conditioned room in lower Manhattan, the tapes contain information on the reading habits of one million Americans."
Look, the *nature* of the contents of those tapes is not in any way related to the place of their storage or the condition of the air there. Therefore the foregoing is not a sensible sentence. The following one would be:
"Recorded over a period of only four weeks at the corner of 42nd Street and Broadway, the tapes contain samples of the dialectal variations of one million Americans."
But of course what you wanted to convey were the several bits of information in the first example above. All right, if you *must* put those items in the same sentence, do it this way: "The tapes, stored in an air-conditioned room in lower Manhattan, contain information . . ." There *is* a difference.

"Based on solid-state circuitry, this new controller is able to handle heat demands ranging from less than 1 per cent of capacity to full on."

The truth is that the fact that it employs solid-state circuitry is not at all responsible for this instrument's wide range of heat-handling ability. An older type of circuitry could do the same thing. But the quoted sentence plainly credits the solid-state circuitry with giving the controller its wide range. As a result, we have an actual misstatement arising from addiction to a cliché journalese construction.

"Women have made up their minds about wanting the extra bathroom. Although generally of small dimensions, the housewife has found it more than pays . . ."
Some of the best housewives *we* know are of quite substantial dimensions.

"Born at Glens Falls, N.Y., Horton received his early art training at Hillsdale College in Michigan." (This makes it sound as though Hillsdale were the obvious and logical college for a Glens Falls, N.Y. native.)

"Worn on a chain with swivel and button, this model retails at $39.95." (But how much'll you charge me, Sir, if I just carry it loose in my pocket?)

"After setting foot on the uninhabited island of Europa, off Africa, to direct the filming of sea turtles, a hurricane wheeled across the Indian ocean and hit the island."
Many a hurricane could be said to leave its footprints, figuratively, but few of them are talented enough to direct a film.

"Designed by the Caloric appliance people, this dispenser can be built into the wall or mounted on the surface." . . . Written by a careless writer, this kind of sentence should not be built into anything.

Trying Too Hard

"Communications with potential customers can be virtually hamstrung just by the complexity of names of the materials."

Figurative language is fine, but *hamstrung* is not an appropriate figure in such a context. Generally speaking, the presence of several figurative expressions of questionable appropriateness in a piece of writing gives the impression that the writer is "trying too hard," an almost fatal failing in any artistic endeavor.

"We should stop this willy-nilly spreading of our dollars over more than 100 countries . . ."

Well, now, "willy-nilly" may sound as though it's quite akin to "helter-skelter," "higgledy-piggledy" and "hit-or-miss," but actually it has two distinct meanings, each quite different from the meaning intended in the quote above. Look it up.

"With a little imagination you, too, can turn out recipes to delight a gourmet. The 'coup de grâce' is using wine in your cooking."

That is, if you're Lucrezia Borgia.

THE ICEBERG SYNDROME—Often a writer tries to give his prose a mildly scientific tone by comparing a problem or a situation to an iceberg, in that there is a great deal more below the surface than appears above it. Of course there is nothing wrong with this, in general terms, but too often the speaker or writer is not content to say it in general terms, and in the process of tossing off a reference to the invisible fraction of the iceberg he betrays the fact that he's never been very close to one. The big trouble with this is, of course, that one or two members of the audience may really know what that fraction is, and the speaker's (or writer's) mentioning the wrong number will cause at least a momentary distraction from the main point he's trying to make, if not downright and continuing distrust.

So, if you must use the iceberg reference—and it's not a very distinguished one, anyway—try to remember: encyclopedias generally agree that "about one-ninth" of the berg's total mass is visible above the sea. That leaves eight-ninths of it submerged. Don't forget!

DETOUR DE FORCE—"We'd like to have stockholders and analysts regard this company as an unique tour de force in consumer marketing. . . ."

Oops! The writer was, consciously or un, seeking to execute a tour de force in phrase-making but succeeded only in producing a detour de force. The single word "force" was what he meant.

Also, make it "*a* unique." Would you say, "I watched an youth chop down an yew tree"? Or "He wanted to enroll in an university"?

"Mr. Rothschild is the type of man Shakespeare had in mind when he said: 'Age cannot wither nor custom stale his infinite variety'."

A Little Literariness is a Dangerous Thing. Shakespeare had the smoothness not to say such a softly poetic thing about a man, but about Cleopatra, an intensely feminine female.

Of course, there was an actual misquotation ("his" instead of "her"), but that error in gender of pronoun is less significant than the broader one of inappropriateness. . . . On second thought, this might not have been too out of place if Mr. Rothschild were a concert pianist or violinist—or harpist or painter—and we were talking about the variety of his artistry, but that was not the case.

Of course the real trouble with a misused figurative word or phrase is not merely that it fails to make the point you wanted to make-with-a-flourish; with many a knowing reader it back-fires as well as misfires because he catches you in a bit of literary pretentiousness.

TAKE A QUANTUM JUMP, AND—

"We anticipate a quantum jump in imports in the next two years."

If he means a very large jump, a substantial jump, a 42 per cent jump, why doesn't he say so? Except in the very largest of dictionaries there is nothing to indicate that it refers to a particularly *large* amount; the connotation is mainly a *specified* amount (quantum = how much?).

Beware faddism in words. One shouldn't try to write the way engineers and scientists do unless he is indeed an engineer or scientist—and even then he should try to sound as little like one as possible, unless he's writing for fellow engineers or scientists.

Another locution, somewhat older, of a same type is "order of magnitude." Even engineers are not unanimous in explaining just what this means, though many assume that it means, roughly, "10 times as much." So why not say it so that there is as little doubt as possible *what* the "magnitude" of the difference is?

Non Sequiturs

"One of the oldest of building materials, ceramic tile comes in various sizes and shapes."

A lot of old things, such as old people, come in various sizes and shapes, too—but its antiquity is not what gives *tile its* variety of shapes. There is, however, a way in which this inverted-phrase locution *would* make sense, to wit: "One of the oldest of building materials, ceramic tile is available today in sizes and shapes adaptable to the most modern of treatments."

"The man who directs the Blank organization is a big, hearty six-footer who looks far younger than his 59 years. But *even* in 1933 he was no stranger to the business." (Because, even then, he was six feet tall, eh?)

Last line of story about Anna Jarvis, founder of Mother's Day: "A tall, red-haired beauty, she never married."

CAUSE AND EFFECT—"He had the hard job of selling tin shingles in an area where the main industry was manufacturing pine shingles. So successful was he that many buildings in the area today are still roofed with the tin shingles he sold." (Huh-uh. He was successful and sold a lot of shingles—but the fact that those shingles have lasted so long is a tribute to their quality, not his salesmanship.)

"Because breath is so vital to life," Burmeister explained, "the field of inhalation therapy and the development of breathing equipment has become *increasingly* important in medical science today."

It may be true that these things are *increasingly* important, but not because breath is vital to life. Breath was just as important to life 3,000 years ago as it is today.

"Called Moonglitter, the new material was invented by a schoolteacher in Oklahoma." . . . "Called Permastain, the paint is a product of Sherman-Dillings." . . . "Called Aphrodite, the perfume is made from imported caraway seed and Indiana wintergreen." . . . Called Writing, these sentences are non sequiturs.

"Open to building owners, managers, architects and engineers, the exhibit shows how automation can pay for itself by saving time and money."

Such an approach would be okay if the sentence were saying that the exhibit shows something instantly recognizable as being of special interest to those particular invitees. For example: "Open to Boy Scouts and scoutmasters, the exhibit shows how infrared pocket stoves are better than rubbing two sticks together." . . . Incidentally, the words "by saving time and money" add practically nothing to the idea already conveyed by the phrase "pay for itself." If it paid for itself in some nonusual benefits—that is, by something *other than* savings in time and money— *that* would deserve mentioning.

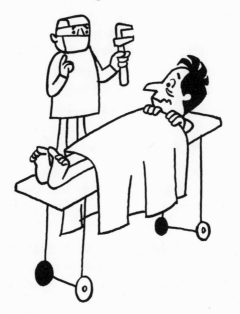

COLUMBUS, Ohio.—About 400 workers at the Blackstone Company have been laid off temporarily for retooling, President Jones said. . . .

Social Security, Old-Age Benefits—and now, this!

Arithmetic

A Quiz

EXAMPLE 1:

First-quarter sales were four times higher than for the first quarter of the previous year.

First-quarter sales were four times as high as for the first quarter of the previous year.

Are those two sentences synonymous? Yes or no.   *no*

EXAMPLE 2:

Earnings this year were 150 per cent over last year's.

Earnings this year were 150 per cent of last year's.

Are those two sentences synonymous? Yes or no.

EXAMPLE 3:

The Explorer capsule is two-and-a-half times larger than Titan.

The Explorer capsule is three-and-a-half times as large as Titan.

Do these two sentences convey to you the *same* information *yes* about the relative size of the two capsules, or *different* information?

Before peeking at the answers (see page 55) you may wish to read this illustration of the principle involved:

If Bill has four apples and Tom has two apples, how would

you describe Bill's relative wealth in apples? Would you not say, "Bill has twice *as many* apples *as* Tom"? Would anyone write: "Bill has twice *more* apples *than* Tom"?

Now, suppose the figures on apples were six and two instead of four and two. Why should one then change from the straightforward language used before and say: "Bill has three times *more* apples than Tom"?

Now the answers to the three numbered examples: The answer to 1 is no; 2 it is also no; to 3 it's same information.

It sometimes is argued that it "doesn't make any difference" whether you say sales this week were four times *higher than* or four times *as high as* (when the cash register reading is 400 to 100). The contention is that the general public regards the two ways of saying it as synonymous, that the "times *higher*" or "times *more*" has attained the status of idiom.

This, sad to say, is probably true. The "maximization" language so long dinned into our ears by hard-sell commercial messages has undeniably had its effect.

But there is an absolutely decisive reason why writers in public relations especially do not dare fall into this particular area of idiomatic use, an area where loose language makes unreliable, or downright misleading, the statistics being attributed to a client's business or product ("three times more cleaning power!"). . . . That reason is that the editors who have the power of life or death over our offerings are just the type who will recognize when imprecise wordage is being used with such statistics and will resent and distrust it, especially since this kind of looseness invariably errs on the side of exaggeration. This, the reaction of the editors, plays a key role in the elementary matter of acceptance of public relations material.

Gee-ometry

"First, a committee selects an area 6 miles in a circle."

You hear it said occasionally that a person can be "good in

English but terrible in arithmetic." But it certainly does no harm for a writer, particularly a writer of expository material, to have at least a clear head for basic arithmetic. And, in the case above, it would have helped if he'd understood the relationships of radius, diameter and circumference!

Another Inexact Specification: "This new drone has a reconnaissance capability within a several mile radius."

More evidence that lack of awareness about basic arithmetical realities can hurt the quality of one's rhetoric: ". . . I would estimate the chances as about one-fourth of one per cent out of a hundred."

". . . if they'd follow this plan they could increase business upwards to 50 per cent."
1. What other direction than up could an increase go?
2. The writer probably meant to convey the information that business could be increased *by an amount* up to 50 per cent greater than had prevailed. Or possibly he meant business could be increased by an amount "upwards *of*" 50 per cent (that is, at least 50 per cent and probably more).
The main point is that the reader cannot be sure *what* the writer meant.

Higher Mathematics

News item: "Elliott Roosevelt announced last night that beginning at 8 a.m. Saturday he would start selling 50,000 to 65,000 Christmas trees in three vacant Manhattan lots at prices he estimated would be from 200 to 300 per cent below the New York retail list."
Pretty generous.

MADEMATICS: "This will be an *increase* of about 50,000 *more* starts than in 1961 and . . ." That's redundant, ungrammatical,

ambiguous. Why not simply "This will be about 50,000 more starts than there were in 1961 and . . ."? If it's an increase it has to be more than—and vice versa.

REDUCED OVER?—"The textile industry reduced errors in advertising by 33 per cent over the previous year, according to a study . . ."

Too bad it didn't reduce its errors in describing a reduction as being "over" the thing reduced.

Percentages of Percentages —Danger!

"The Administration had asked for only a 5 per cent cut in the existing 10 per cent tax on new autos."

This would bring the new tax to 9½ per cent.

But the writer did not mean that. He meant to say that what the administration had asked for was that the 10 per cent tax on new autos be dropped to 5 per cent (or cut in half).

Mentioning a percentage of a percentage is always tricky. If, for instance, 30 per cent of the kids in a given schoolhouse had dental cavities last year, but this year, after a conscientious, scientific, etc., program of dental care only 25 per cent are thus afflicted, the improvement is not one of 5 per cent fewer cavity-havers, but of 16.66 per cent (5/30 or 1/6) fewer.

A good approach is to convert (mentally) the first set of percentage figures into "index numbers"; that is, just regard them as index numbers, and then make a brand-new percentage calculation based on their relation to each other. Furthermore, when you get the new percentage, tell about it in *times as many* or in *fractions* to minimize confusion with the first percentage reference.

"Factory orders for durable goods fell to a *seasonally adjusted* $23.1 billion in August, down 4.5 per cent from July."

You cannot *adjust*, seasonally or otherwise, a flat figure that has already been achieved. You can have seasonally adjusted *indexes*, or *expectations*, but statistics that have happened have happened, period.

Ten Public Enemies

Cliché Alphabet

A man reviewing a book in the *Saturday Review* commented that "we are a nation devoted to clichés because we are enchanted by labor-saving devices, *and the cliché is the greatest labor-saving device ever invented by man: it eliminates the necessity for thought.*"

This gives us the excuse to lay before thinking writers a sort of check list of cliché phrases, words or tactics that raise their ugly heads (oops!—and, for that matter, oops for the oops!) once in a not-too-great while in the copy stream.

It should be made crystal clear (see below) that the following cataloging of clichés is not meant to imply that every entry is unforgivably and invariably to be condemned. Some of them are quite okay in certain contexts. The borderline ones are listed here just as a reminder that when you find yourself starting to write one you should give it a second thought and ask yourself if this really says exactly what you want to say or if you just reached for it out of habit?

announcement—as in "in making the announcement, President Jones"
asserted—unless you're deliberately trying to make your man sound pompous, "said" is probably the better verb
as you know

baptism of fire
bare minimum
beams approval—a photo caption horror; akin to "looking on," q.v.
breakthrough—use sparingly, preferably only in direct quotation, and preferably *never* in lead sentence

cherchez—la femme, whom else?
chilly—as in "on the mountain top it was a chilly 30 below zero"
crystal clear

declared, declaring—seldom does a man's manner of saying something warrant this instead of just plain "said"
dollars and sense

expertise—most of the time "expertness" is what you really mean

foreseeable future—not really bad, but avoid overuse

Frankenstein (that destroys its maker)—Frankenstein WAS the maker, not the monster!

goofed—as in "We goofed"; even worse, in a note sending a correction: "Is our face red?"

grinds to a halt

hopefully—beware of using this adverb in such a way as to impute the capacity for "hoping" to some utterly inanimate object

in his new position
in no uncertain terms
in order to
importantly—the -ly is unnecessary and erroneous in "and, more importantly—"

J—Anybody know one?

K—Or for this, either?

the ladies, God bless 'em—
legion (their name is; or their number is)
like a cigarette (or anything else) should—
lion's share—
lo, these many years—
looking on—verboten in a caption

Milady
more importantly, most importantly—see above re giving the lie
  to -ly.
mousetrap—beware also better mousetrap, proverbial mousetrap,
  proverbial better mousetrap; be sure you are aware of what
  made that mousetrap so proverbial if you're tempted to use
  the term.

note—as in "it is interesting to . . ."

of course—be careful not to use it too often in an effort to create
  an atmosphere of sweet reasonableness

pointed out—be sure that what this refers to is something that
  logically could be "pointed out," not some fact never before
  known to anyone

pretty Mabel Thrush, etc. (in caption)—gratuitous; let the reader
  decide for himself whether she's pretty or not

proves conclusively—

queried—asked or questioned might do just as well . . . maybe
  better

revolutionary—use sparingly; double-sparingly, in a lead sentence

staggering—as in "staggering sum of . . ." see also *thumping, whopping*

swoop—as in "one fell ____"; spoonerizing it doesn't help, either; probably makes it worse

thought—as in "Thought you'd like to read this speech by our president"

thumping (see also *staggering, whopping*)

to my knowledge—the Turnquote's Best Friend

unique—use sparingly, especially in lead sentence; also, be sure the thing so described is, literally, unique.

venture—as in "venture an opinion"

vital—not as vital an adjective as some people think it is

whopping—as in "Sales were up a whopping 46 per cent." Let the figures tell the story. If they are staggering, or thumping, enough to deserve the adjective, the reader probably will be as aware of it as the writer.

without fear of successful contradiction

without further ado

woefully weak—*that it is.*

X, Y, Z—they mark three spots yet to be filled

P.S. To the Surprise of No One, the cliché parade Struck a Nerve and sparked a Prompt Reaction. The several gaps in the abecedarian array obviously Posed a Challenge that proved irresistible to many Cooler Heads.

For *J* there was a Veritable Avalanche of suggestions, among them: Just desserts, Jealously guarded, Just for the record, Jaundiced eye. For *K:* Knockdown and drag out, Kill-or-cure treatment, King's ransom.

Lest any of us get carried away and become so self-conscious about this that we can hardly write straight because of cliché-phobia, it should again be made Crystal Clear, Like the Man Said, that we do not have to Shun every such phrase Like the Plague. Not all of them are All Bad in every situation. It's just that we should be on guard against using too many of them, or using any one too often or thoughtlessly or in a coy or smarty-pants way (Dollars and *Sense*).

Helpful Headlines

Everybody knows what headlines are, but not everybody feels the same about headlines. There are different types of headlines, and different reactions to them.

A theory held by some public relations folk is that there is a risk in putting a head on a publicity release; namely that it may be regarded by newspaper people as presumptuous. We feel this is being unnecessarily diffident, and that the various advantages of having headlines far outweigh that marginal hazard.

There is one other hazard in headlines, though: headlines with unrealistically long unit counts remind the editors that the writer is indifferent to, or ignorant of, the realities of headlines-type limitations.

So the advice is: If you are going to put headlines on your releases, couched in true "headlinese," be sure to hold down the unit count. Otherwise, use a "label" type of heading.

As for clever headlines on a feature story, long or short: there may be a hazard in getting too cute, but there is more to be gained than lost if you can devise a head capable of attracting an editor's attention (even if he moans a little).

Here are a few examples:

POLISH MAKER AIMS TO PLEASE,
MAKES POLISH PLEASING TO AIM

(about a new, easy-to-use shoe-polish dispenser)

MAKING A CLICHÉ CLICK. Sometimes it is possible to take the curse off a cliché phrase by giving it a twist that capitalizes upon its very clichédom. On a story about a new use of ultrasonics for ascertaining whether an expectant mother is going to have twins, a scribe who was understandably fed up with the "tennis, any-one?" fad phrase came up with:

DOUBLES, ANYONE?

**SKIERS CAN BET THEIR BOOTS
ON THESE SHOE-CARE TIPS**

**CHAIN SAWS CAN DO A GOOD TURN
DAILY AT BOY SCOUT CAMP SITES**

**DAD'S BEARISH?
GIVE HIM A DEN**
(story suggesting a "home office" be set up for Dad)

The summer following the college basketball "dumping" scandal in New York there was a formal inquiry into allegations that it was in some of the summer resorts in the Catskills, where athletes doubled as bus boys and basketball performers at higher-than-busboy wages, that the gamblers had made contact with key players in the plot. The *World-Telegram*'s headline summed it up:

**HOTEL MEN DENY CHARGE
CREAM IN BORSCHT BELT
MADE CAGERS TURN SOUR**

Check and Double Check

It is by no means desirable to reduce all writing from a given shop, or person, to a formula. However, sometimes formulas serve a constructive purpose, especially when they are used as a measuring stick or check list. If you use the following array of check points occasionally to see how a thing you have written fulfills some of these basic conditions, you may develop an automatic, somewhat subconscious checking system that'll help you get the most out of yourself and out of any news situation you are dealing with.

I. Since a story, to be newsworthy, has to include at least one of the following, ask yourself if yours does.

1. Is it information anyone would likely repeat to a neighbor over a back fence or a bridge table?

2. Is it amusing?

3. Does it convey anything unexpected or out of the ordinary?

4. Is it the viewpoint of an important person?

II. Have you made it sound as though something has happened —or is going to happen?

III. If you're quoting anybody:

1. Does it sound like something Vice President McCartwheel actually might have said—or like something a publicitor would invent?

2. Does it sound like anything anybody might ever say?

3. Invent something yourself—if you can make it good—a simile, a metaphor . . . but still make it sound as though the man might have said it.

IV. Have you distorted what would be the normal sequence of ideas to get the plug in higher up than it would otherwise be? . . . If you have, work it over some more—not to move the plug down but to make it fit naturally and without throwing other elements of the story out of balance.

V. Have you written the story in active instead of passive terms so far as possible? (That is, have you written "The Blank company weighed the advantages of seven cities before locating in Middleport," or "Consideration was given by the Blank company to the advantages . . ."?)

VI. Have you made the story as "personal" as possible? Of

course you're aware that "names make news," but let's remember also that items that put the accent on what is happening to people (named or not) have much more appeal than those that by the very impersonality of their language fail to make the reader think of the event in terms of people.

VII. Have you used any mannered, trite, albeit perhaps "fashionable" words or phrases just out of sheer habit of "writing like a writer" instead of writing like a person telling another person something?

Write What You Mean

News editors try to discourage use of the cliché "to my knowledge" because it is either thoughtlessly vague or deliberately equivocal (pretending to intensify a statement but leaving a loophole if one proves to be needed). Here is an example that may rate as the all-time tops in use of an emphasizer that doesn't emphasize:

To our knowledge *nobody* has *any* reason to believe that the factual reporting of those elections has caused any Western voters to jump on a bandwagon or stay at home . . .

USE-CARE-WITH-QUOTES Note: "A major company announced today that it has joined the 'forward-looking' minority of U.S. firms that pay the full cost of group health insurance for employees."

Quoting just the adjective, as was done above, implies cynicism as to whether the firms really are forward-looking. This is just the reverse of the back-patting implication that was intended. Solution? Be content to let the facts win appreciation for the progressiveness of the company.

"Due to the urgency of settling the railroad dispute, observers contend that the committee will halt hearings on the other matter."

The foregoing sentence states that the action of observers (namely, contending) was *due to* the urgency of settling, etc. This is not a true statement. There are several ways of saying this in a way that avoids misstatement—which springs from not recognizing the difference between "said that" and "said":

1. Observers contend that, because of the urgency of settling the railroad dispute, the committee will halt hearings on the other matter.

2. Because of the urgency of settling the railroad dispute, observers contend, the committee will halt . . .

3. The need to settle the railroad dispute has such priority, observers say, that the committee is sure to halt . . .

WRONG OR—"The picnicker has no alternative between carrying disposable items on his person or throwing them away wherever he is."

"Alternative" is a Word to Watch Out For. Use of it calls for appreciation of the difference that can be made by nonperceptive use of such uncomplicated little words as "or" and "between" and "of" and "to" and "and."

Did Homer write that Odysseus faced the perilous task of sailing "between Scylla or Charybdis"? No, he didn't. Does the stern Saturday-morning parent say to his son: "You have no alternative between raking the lawn or washing the car"?

At the restaurant, you might have "a choice *of* apple or huckleberry pie." But if you are invited to make a choice *between* them, then it's between apple *and* huckleberry.

PLAYING IT BY EAR

A reporter on a small Oklahoma newspaper turned in a story that had been phoned in by a farmer in the area, about a big fire. The city editor was astounded at the size of the livestock loss, reported at 2,025 cows. The reporter had left the office, so the editor himself telephoned the farm to check it out. "Are you the man who had the fire that wiped out 2,025 cows?" inquired the editor. "Yeth," replied the farmer.

Whereupon the editor grabbed his pencil and did a bit of significant copyreading on the dispatch, substantially reducing the number of animals lost. Can you figure what he did? Clue: total number of animals that perished was 27.

BORN TO THE JOB: "Dr. Rengler has been technical director of the division since inception."

'TWAS EVER THUS DEPT.: "With an eye cocked on the fair sex, designers and builders are giving it an important place in home remodeling."

VERSATILE MACHINE: "The fluoroscopic system makes moving pictures and tape recordings of the mouth and throat while speaking, chewing and swallowing." . . . Probably patting its head and rubbing its tummy at the same time, too.

"Nearly every year for many years thereafter he repeated his call for a change in the injustice of that law. . . ."
Wanted his own kind of injustice, eh?

FLATTERER! A news story identified a lady doctor as "a recognized veteran in microbiology." Not a very convincing description, and, especially for a lady, not a flattering one. She probably likes being recognized as an authority or expert, but it's a rare lady who would be pleased to be reminded that her veteranship is recognizable.

"Today Americans eat more pizzas than Italians."
But they gradually are acquiring a taste for the latter. (Make it "than *the* Italians *do*.")

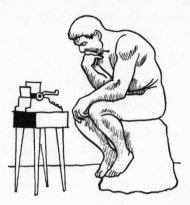

BEWARE OF HITCH-HIKERS. Resist the temptation to "hitch-hike" a *who* or *whom* phrase onto a sentence that is sufficient unto itself, just to tack on an added item of information.

EXAMPLE:

> To relax, Mr. Choate likes to take in a ball game or a good show with his wife—both of whom, of course, enjoy a glass of good wine to top off a pleasant evening.

Why not let the second idea stand as a sentence by itself: "Both of them enjoy . . ."? (And, by the way, how did that patronizing "of course" get in there, anyway?)

DIFFERENT . . . ?—"Different than" is generally frowned upon by those who pay close attention to what they write—and what they read. Here is a brief natural-history note that illustrates how "different from" is different from "different than":

Both a man and a dog are different from a wolf, but a man is more different than a dog.

Leads with a Lilt

"Sometimes a rainy day necessitates invention by a mother."

"If your cat catnaps on top of the piano, chances are you are in for a chilly winter" (story about desirability of zoned heat control in a home).

"The Southern Pacific Railroad, which for 60 years has been watching its switches, is now switching its watches" (approved electronic wristwatches).

"What makes Anna wink?
"It takes a lot more than plain flirtatiousness to induce a wink from Anna, the geodetic 'firefly' satellite, according to Bendix Corporation engineers."

"Hallowe'en may bring out the goblins and ghosts, but in many homes it's likely to turn up something even more shivery—a heating system that's only a shadow of its former self."

"Every car-driving mother should know one more thing about the birds and the bees. Especially lady drivers. And even more especially, lady drivers with their children aboard." (What they should know is that birds and bees and other insects cause highway accidents; so stop the car as quickly as possible if one flies in.)

"The failure to stop for a nap is the last mistake many drivers ever make."

A general football story on a particular Saturday morning in November when Harvard was to play Yale; Notre Dame was meeting Michigan State; California was at Stanford, Indiana at Purdue, etc., etc., had this lead by Allison Danzig:
"Today the name of the game is 'THE.' "

"For some reason the feel of a wheel turns many a pedestrian Jekyll into a highway Hyde."

"Ten years from now we'll all be so comfortable at home that

we won't even know it" (lead on a story about the scientific
theory that only when one is at least somewhat uncomfortable
does he have any awareness of *whether* he's warm enough or
cool enough).

"Such a house [30 years old or more], if it doesn't suffer from
hardening of the plumbing arteries or sclerosis of the heating
system, is likely to fall victim to *culinary thrombosis* or laundry
letdown."

"The country's railroads, long regarded as the backbone of the
nation's transportation system, are about ready to take their
aching backbone to an osteopath."

"CLYDE, O.—A sauerkraut processor here has found an easy
way to save cabbage—the kind you spend as well as the kind
you eat. He merely substituted plastic sheets for the loose
wooden lids that cover his large fermentation vats."
The above was translated from:
"CLYDE, O.—Once again polyvinyl chloride, the workhouse
plastic of industry and home, makes possible a new concept in
the manufacture of an age-old produce, this time sauerkraut."

"Mark Twain said everybody does two things he dislikes every
day: go to bed, and get up." (Lead on story on behalf of automatic thermostats that turn heat down at night, up in the
morning.)

"Trips to the moon are hard on a home. So are rodeos.
"But a family's space cadets and cowboys are still lovable even
if their energies sometimes make the walls of a room shudder.
To ease it, give them more room."

"You won't be able to keep a snake in the grass once he's seen
the new Bronx Zoo—thanks to automatically controlled radiant

heat." (The heat made the concrete warmer "out front," coaxing the heat-seeking reptiles out where the public could see them better.)

"But no sooner does the Little Woman pull into the new Vacant Acres Shopping Center's parking lot than she starts asking *in a foot-tapping tone of voice* how soon the next bus to the stores will be along."

"There's no present like the time" (story suggesting a watch for a Christmas gift, especially for a friend who's often tardy).

"People have studied computers for years; now computers are studying people."
This lead also illustrates an effective use of the much-neglected semicolon. The phrases might have been linked via comma and either "but" or "and." But the semicolon does it better than either of those would.

From a story on the ups and downs of the plumbing business: "Then a dark ring settled on the bathtub picture during the postwar period. Soaring costs and the trend to smaller homes pulled the plug on the tub market so that . . ."

LILTING ALLITERATION—". . . openings are more likely to be available at Southern, Midwestern and Western schools and at 'new' colleges than at prestige schools (mostly in the East) whose campuses are *eaves-deep in ivy*."

"Someone once said that the latest thing in clothes is generally the woman you are waiting for."

"LOS ANGELES—Early Bird, the world's first commercial communications satellite, was hatched six weeks ahead of schedule here today."

Variations on a Theme of Hyphen

"The company instituted an anti-stream pollution campaign."

Literally, this says the company started a pollution campaign against streams. Better say ". . . instituted an anti-stream-pollution campaign." Still better: ". . . instituted an anti-pollution campaign." (The context would make it clear that it is streams that are to be saved from pollution.)

". . . the new hospital has spot lighting to give plenty of illumination to a late reader while letting his bed-neighbor go to sleep." (In a hospital? What he meant was *next-bed* neighbor.)

"Lake Redwing has been a favorite resort for years because of its low humidity, its dust and smog-free air."

Yes sir, the dust is delightful there, eh? The writer meant "its low humidity *and* its dust- and smog-free air."

A small item carrying information for do-it-yourselfers on *how*

to accomplish a certain household task in a labor-saving manner bore the headline: "How to Tip." The absence of the required hyphen there made it sound, instead, like an item from the etiquette editor—or the drinking editor.

"Subsequently he was responsible for the introduction of fixed price contracts."
Unless the "he" above was a swindler, what he introduced were *fixed-price* contracts.

A piece of illogical punctuation has taken root in business-news releases and is now widely used. For example, "Joe Doakes has been elected vice president-engineering of the Soandso Company." "Robert Roakes was named vice president-sales for the Eastern district."
A sensible way to eschew this affront to all hyphen appreci-ators is simple transposition, so that such persons are identified as "engineering vice president," "sales vice president" and so on. . . . However, if there is absolute insistence upon using that form, there is a typographic compromise that some have found useful, namely, the use of a dash (on the typewriter, two hyphens end to end) but without the customary spacing appro-prite to a regular, conventional dash.

What's wrong with this headline?

NURSE ATTACKED
BY HATCHET
BRANDISHING MAN

Whichcraft

"The house that Jack built" holds one of the most mnemonical keys to keeping clearly in mind the difference between those bothersome clause-introducers THAT and WHICH.

Grammar books tell us to remember that one of these is used in a "nonrestrictive" clause, the other in a "restrictive" one. But most people find it hard to remember whether *which* goes with *that* clause, or *that* goes with *which* clause—not to mention the difficulty of being sure what makes a clause *restrictive* and what makes it *nonrestrictive*.

So let's just try these contrasting examples:

1. This is the house *that* Jack built.
BUT
    This house, *which* Jack built with the aid of his neighbors, is the prettiest one on the block.

2. The river *that* separates Manhattan from Jersey is the Hudson.
BUT
    The Hudson river, *which* separates Manhattan from Jersey, is muddier than the Gowanus canal, *which* is in Brooklyn.

3. The Douglas transport *that* has two engines is the DC-3.
BUT
The Douglas DC-3, *which* has two engines, is held in high esteem for its "workhorse" capabilities.

Most people with an ear for words agree that *that* is a faster, "smoother" word than *which*. It lets a sentence flow better.

This leads us to a final mnemonic, based upon the rhyming relationship of WHICH and HITCH. Refer again to the three examples above, and note that in each sentence "where there's a '*hitch*' (clause set off in commas) there's a *which*."

P.S. If you doubt the assertion that *that* is faster and smoother than *which,* you might try reading the full text (11 lines) of the *House That Jack Built* jingle, substituting *which* for each of the 12 *thats* therein. See how it sounds.

There is a tendency on the part of some news writers to use "which" as a connective to hook a second idea onto a sentence that does not need any second thoughts.
EXAMPLE:
And things will get worse before they get better, predicts the Federal Aviation Agency, *which* estimates that as much as 60 per cent of the airline patron's time is spent on the ground, depending on the length of his journey.

Why not end the first sentence after "Agency," then come up with a new one: "It estimates ; . ."? You'd have two fairly impressive statements, all the more impressive because of standing alone, and much less of a mouthful for the reader.

The same thing is true of ". . . program that resulted in the first electronic watch for consumers, *which* was later adapted for use as a timing device for satellites." Again, each of these points would be made more emphatic by your putting them in separate sentences.

WHOSE—The dictionary definition of "whose" is: "the possessive case of *who*, and now, usually, of *which*." So you do not need to feel you are being in the slightest ungrammatical, or inelegant, or impure, in using such a construction as "she arrived in a French automobile *whose* upholstery was pure Louis 14th." In fact, it is unnecessarily roundabout, clumsy and sometimes even misleading (at least momentarily) to use the other construction, that is, "arrived in a French automobile, the upholstery of which, etc."

VIVE LA DIFFERENCE!—"One thing is clear; every country *that* has progressed technologically and has developed an industrial economy has had a patent incentive system. But, strangely enough, industry, *which* relies on patent protection and actually pays most of the bill, has neglected to make its interests clearly heard."

The above is an example of correct differentiation. Note the "hitch" that gives the clue to the "which" clause.

Who or Whom?

Who among us would not be grateful for a quick, easy and foolproof way of deciding whether to use *who* or *whom* in certain troublesome clauses?

Ted Bernstein of *The New York Times* offers a neat test (in his book *The Careful Writer*).

You simply convert the clause into a straightaway sentence that says the same thing, substituting a *personal* pronoun (he or him, she or her) for the *relative* one (who or whom), and you can see instantly whether the who-or-whom should be in the *nominative* or the *objective* case.

EXAMPLE:

Bill Russell, *whom* Red Auerbach characterized as the greatest defensive genius the game has ever known, yesterday was named coach of the Celtics.

In the suggested conversion you would say, "Auerbach characterized *him* . . ."; therefore, use *whom*.

But if the original sentence were "Bill Russell, *who* Red Auerbach said was the greatest defensive genius . . . ," your conversion would read "Auerbach said *he* was the greatest . . ."; therefore, use *who*.

Another version of the original sentence might be "Bill Russell, *who* was characterized *by* Red Auerbach. . . ." In that event your conversion would be "*He* was characterized by Auerbach . . . ," so, again, use *who*.

It is possible to concoct a similar rationale on *whoever* vs. *whomever*, but it requires meticulous logic of almost Ph.D. proportions. So we are going to take refuge in a paraphrase, "discretion is the better part of grammar," and advise simply that unless you have no doubt whatever about which case is called for ("*Whoever* told you that?" . . . "I'll dance with *whomever* I please!"), you'll make your readers as well as yourself happier if you just *recast the sentence*. Duck it. You'll live to write again another day.

Will Power vs. Shall Power

"Where there's a *shall* there's a *will*."

That twist on the old maxim about a will's being able to find a way capsulizes what seems to be happening to the old will-shall/would-should balance of power.

A couple of generations ago the "rule" that all of us struggled with and some managed to learn was: To express simple future intent or plans, use *shall* in the first person, *will* in the second and third persons . . . and to express a vow, utter a command or declare firm determination you simply reversed things. Remembering the format of those "*Thou shalt* nots" of the Ten Commandments helped us keep things reasonably straight.

But in recent years those precepts have been fading steadily, probably because they seemed to be quite arbitrary and without any readily recognized basis in logic. Even well-lettered people nowadays do not seem to be making distinctions between first and second or third persons, using *will* almost always in routine mentions of something that's going to happen or be done, and resorting to *shall* only when they're being quite formal or quite emphatic—or, indeed, quite determined.

EXAMPLES:

"I shall return," said General MacArthur upon leaving Corregidor.

"We Shall Overcome," sing the Freedom Marchers.

"We shall fight on the beaches, in the streets . . . we shall never surrender," declared Sir Winston Churchill.

Conclusion: Don't fret about it. Let the "sound" and the context be your guide. And, as a final comforter, note that if you put any phrases involving this problem into the contracted form (increasingly allowable), you can escape any liability, because the contractions are defined as representing either will or shall, should or would. Viz.: *I'd* climb the highest mountain; *I'll* be seeing you; *you'll* never walk alone; *he'd* never beat me in a 15-round fight.

Tense Sense

All of us were brought up to remember that in indirect discourse if you used the past tense for the verb of saying (he *said, declared, promised, explained,* etc.) you had to use either the past tense or the conditional form for the ensuing verb, as: "He *said* he *was* tired of the endless bickering." Or "He *explained* he *would* have no hesitation in challenging Mount McKinley because . . ."

Some learned that lesson too positively. There are exceptions, and in recent years the tendency is to make exceptions in more cases, not to be too firmly bound by the rule of "past follows past." The basic exception always has been that you use the present tense if what the man said expresses a timeless idea: "He *said* that the world *is* round." (If one were to use *was* in such a sentence it would hint at the possibility that the world has changed shape.)

Along this same line, one can go to the present tense either where there is a strong idea that a condition still continues in effect or where the use of the past tense (as above) would be ambiguous or misleading. For example, "He pointed out that about one-fourth of the food chain's stores *were* less than five years old." Make it *are*, assuring the reader that this is the situation that does prevail now. . . . "The survey showed that the best credit risk for auto financing, regardless of age or income, *was* the man who has been working for one employer 15 years or more." Again, make it *is*, because it is a continuing situation.

Another example: "The earnings picture, he said, *was* clouded by such factors as . . ." Actually this clouded condition is a continuing one, not something that "*was*." So adhering to the old indirect-discourse rule creates an ambiguity, if not indeed an inaccuracy.

V.

Downstream Ripples

Affect and Effect

Mnemonics is one approach to the problem of remembering the respective roles played by those perennial puzzlers, AFFECT and EFFECT:

1. "The climate of Arizona AFFECTS most people's sinuses favorably" (*affects* = *a*cts upon). But "The EFFECT of six months in Arizona's dry climate was readily apparent" (*effect* = *e*nd result).

2. "The good secretary is not AFFECTED by a boss' profanities [*affected* = *a*cted upon] but sticks to business and EFFECTS a harmonious relationship" (*effects* = brings about an *e*nd result).

3. "The debutante AFFECTED boredom [*affected* = put on *a*irs] but the EFFECT [*effect* = *e*nd result] was, instead, boredom for the young men she was trying to impress."

Agreement in Number

"About half the cats in this country are eating nearly 600 million pounds of cat food a year; the other half presumably makes do with whatever *it* can find."

Come on, now, it really isn't necessary to be that rigid about the sanctity of a singular subject ("half"). Neither the writer nor the reader is thinking in terms of that "other half" foraging around and begging table scraps as one great big monofelinic unit. They're thinking of them as a lot of cats. So let's just make it "presumably *make* do with whatever *they* can find."

After all, this is grammatically defensible, on the ground that in the second section of that sentence the phrase "of the cats," though absent, is *understood*.

Collective Realism

"It is disturbing to learn that a very large percentage—perhaps a majority—of college graduates *is* not attracted to business as a career."

It is true that the word "percentage," intensified by "majority," is technically the subject in the above sentence, and technically seems to call for the singular verb "is." But it does sound a little absurd—doesn't it?—because the reader is not visualizing this array of graduates *en bloc,* but as individuals, some of whom are attracted to business, many of whom are not. So, feel free to use the verb "are" in such a sentence. It will be less likely to set up a wandering train of thought in your reader's mind than the chemically correct "is." Better still, rephrase it to duck the problem.

This Way Out

You may often be confronted with the awkward situation where you have a phrase starting with a collective noun but ending with an "of" phrase mentioning items very much in the plural— and it's a puzzlement whether to use the singular or plural form of the verb.

EXAMPLES:

A variety of styrofoam shapes *are* available for making decorative bases.

This is not strictly grammatical, because "variety" is the subject. On the other hand, it would be unrealistic to say "is available" because of the proximity of the word "shapes" and the fact that *the shapes* are what you're really talking about. So why not recast the sentence slightly:

Styrofoam is available in many interesting shapes for making . . .

Similarly:

Good community relations *is* necessary for every automobile dealer . . .

Again remembering that discretion is the better part of grammar, take your pick among:

A climate of good community relations is . . .

The cultivation of good community relations is . . .

Preservation of good community relations is . . .

Bad 'By' Lines

WATCH THOSE "BY" LINES: "By providing each gantry with its own individual control system, two different parts can be produced simultaneously if required."

What is doing the "providing"? Not the "two different parts," though that is what the above construction says.

A better way: "Because each gantry has (or has been provided with) its own individual control system, two different parts can . . ."

"By working with larger-diameter drive pins and increased power loads, heavy-duty fastenings can be made to hold weighty vent fans and heat exchangers."

Obscure subject. Who does this "working with"? Better: "Larger-diameter drive pins and increased power *make possible* fastenings *that* can hold . . ."

"By having range and range rate of information provided automatically, the pilot does not need to rely on conventional equipment . . ."

Clumsy. "Because" is often a good replacement in such situations: "*Because* range and range rate informations *are* provided automatically . . ."

Bothersome Boths

BEWARE THE BOTHERSOME BOTHS—"All this gives the reader an insight into Fellini's approach to art and life, both of which are synonymous to him." . . . For generations the all-too-typical high school sports reporter's all-too-typical comment, about a close game, has included the observation that "both teams were evenly matched." Nope! Just make it "THE teams were evenly matched." Thus, let's make the first quotation above read like this: ". . . approach to art and life, which, to him, are synonymous."

A PLAGUE ON BOTH—"Curiously, both shows have a common theme."

This says that both shows have a theme that is common, in the sense of undistinguished. What the writer meant to say was: "Curiously, the two shows have a common theme."

What caused the trouble? "Both." The same thing is true of this sentence. "Both scintillation probes operate and record independently, providing separate scans on opposite sides of the subject." Make it "The two" probes.

"Any change in the policy would have to be by agreement between both the Democrats and the Republicans." Block That Both! The "both" is not merely unnecessary but incongruous in such a context.

From a post-Bowl story: ". . . and when both sides are even, the game can be a good one. Both sides in the Super Bowl were not quite even, but . . ."

Both sides not quite even with *what*?

Both sides were big, strong and fast, yes. But: *The* sides were not quite even.

Comma Complaint

EXAMPLE 1:
To help commemorate this unique event, Mr. Fieldhouse re-
    vealed that his company has withdrawn certain supplies.

Mr. Fieldhouse's *revelation* is *not* the thing that will help commemorate the event, yet *that is what the above sentence says.* Put a comma after "revealed," and delete the "that."

EXAMPLE 2:

To help satisfy the changing market structure and changing consumer tastes in the industry, Mr. Goldberg said his company
is planning . . .

Mr. Goldberg did not say it "to help satisfy," . . . so put that
comma after "said."

Here's an especially obvious illustration of the difference between "said that" and "said": "Failing in these efforts, Jones
said that the company agreed to arbitrate. . . ." The foregoing
says unmistakably that *Jones* failed in certain efforts. But if you
make it read: "Failing in these efforts, Jones said, the company
agreed . . . ," you will be relating the true situation, namely
that it was the company that had failed in those efforts (and
Jones was merely the person who *said*).

(Story on comparative costs of building materials, long term.)
"Over the 60-year life of a building, the study found that savings could amount to. . . ." This says that the study went on for
the 60-year life of the building. Make it "Over the 60-year life
of a building, the study found, savings could. . . ."

COMMA SENSE ABOUT COMMAS

There are many instances where commas are superfluous between adjectives in pairs.

EXAMPLES:

He built a new, $35,000 house.

She liked to lie on the raft and enjoy the cool, South wind.

Up to this time the industry had not been able to produce a satisfactory, low-cost gas.

A steaming, hot bowl of soup is a good way to start the day.

If you telephone that number you'll hear a recorded message
featuring a sexy, female voice.

The Consonantal "H"

Why should we write "an historic event" when we do not write "an hysterical woman"; we do not say "I am going to get an haircut"; we do not say, "he was an habitual smoker"? We *do* say, "an honest man," but not "an high school graduate"; we do not say that the choir sang "an hymn" nor that the movie actor rode "an Honda." . . . Granted, one sees the article *an* preceding the definitely aspirated *historic* quite frequently in reasonably literate writings, but the feeling here is that it is an haffectation and constitutes more of an hindrance than an help.

Eye-Hitting Note

"Foyers lend a gracious touch, appealing not only to the home-maker's sense of hospitality, but the insulation they offer against outside blasts of air, cold or hot, makes sense to the man of the house."

In this one, "appealing" is on the *wrong side* of "not only." Furthermore, the second half of the sentence has nothing to do with graciousness. So the two elements should not have been bracketed, anyway, via the "not only/but also" linkage.

This calls to mind the little exercise of seeing how many ways you can insert the word "only" into the following sentence, and seeing how the meaning changes:

I   HIT   HIM   IN   THE   EYE   YESTERDAY
    (a) I   (b) hit   (c) him   (d) in the
        (e) eye   (f) yesterday (g)

Translation: (a) nobody else hit him; (b) I didn't scratch or bite him or anything else; (c) I didn't hit anybody else; (d) no other part of his anatomy was struck; (e) poor guy had only one, and I hit him in it! (f) as recently as yesterday; (g) not day before yesterday, or any other day, just yesterday.

"For Example"

In efforts to be casual some writers tend to use the "for example" phrase more often than necessary—and, worse, to use it where it serves no useful or logical function. Look, "for example," at the following:

By eliminating the uncertainty of erratic weather the growers are able to develop stronger plants and better flowers. Jones' orchid seedlings, for example, are shipped to such distant points as Australia, Hawaii and South America.

Well, the distance to which they are shipped *may* be related to their strength and quality, but it isn't an "example" of *that* unless set forth in those terms, something like this:

Jones' orchid seedlings, for example, have successfully survived shipments and transplantings to points as distant as Australia.

Fuzzy Subject Referral

"Having precise knowledge of his position enables the operator to minimize the danger of losing his drill during rough weather conditions, causing expensive loss of operating time."

There is fuzziness here about the subject of "causing." It could be (a) the clause "Having precise knowledge"; it could be (b) "the operator"; it could be (c) "the danger of losing his drill" or (d) just "losing his drill." Actually (d) is what the writer meant. . . . Let's remove the ambiguity and streamline it a bit by making it read: ". . . enables the operator to minimize the danger of losing his drill in rough weather, a *mishap that can cause* expensive loss," etc.

"Ill-literally"

Somebody should *literally* start a campaign to preserve the literal meaning of "literally." If we keep on using "literally" in places where what is meant is almost its exact opposite—namely, "figuratively"—pretty soon there will be no word that means what "literally" does, logically, mean. The other week one of our most literate magazines quoted a psychiatrist as observing that "Modern man literally lives in a sexual goldfish bowl." That would be something—wouldn't it?—if he really, literally, did!

Let us be literate about "literally." There is a submarine training unit in operation in the completely land-locked town of Farmingdale, N.Y. A story about the school sessions there makes the observation that, in this facility, "groups of between 12 and 20 submariners are literally 'going to sea' each week."

Nope. You cannot literally go to sea except on the sea. Besides, the fact that quotes were put around the phrase itself repudiates the verb "literally."

NONINTENSIFIER: "There is literally no justification for assuming that the public relations director is responsible for . . ."

What there really is no justification for is using "literally" as a presumed intensifier (i.e., for emphasis) in a sentence that does not raise any question as to whether an utterance is meant to be taken literally *or figuratively*.

"Literally" is NOT in any way synonymous with "absolutely," "positively" or "definitely." Granted, you can find a dictionary that will say, broadmindedly, "used loosely for emphasis." *But not here.*

"The low-cost Caravelle watch has *literally* mushroomed in sales volume."

There's *literally* too much nonliterate use of "literally." A watch cannot possibly literally mushroom except perhaps in a painting by Salvador Dali.

"The vice-chairman of the Senate Ethics Committee said today the panel members '*literally* bent over backwards' to be fair to the Senator . . ."

In fact, they make it a flexible rule to do so.

Man on television interview:

"Our work-opportunity office was so successful that the people were *literally* battering the door down to apply." (Subsequent conversation made it clear that the door had not been physically assaulted in the slightest degree; so they only figuratively battered the door.)

Listen While You Write

He was trying to complete the project in the *fastest amount* of time.

The supervisor does not *maintain* sufficient *attention to* fringe items.

Do these phrases *sound* right? No, they don't. An *amount* cannot be measured in speed or slowness. And you don't *maintain* attention *to . . .* The writer was "not listening" to what he was writing.

MORE EXAMPLES:

(a) He said there had been three times as many contracts obtained in 1962 *compared with* 1961.

(b) The *causes* of this reaction are *due to* excess oxygen.

(c) Hence the competitive situation shifts, not only between competing firms but *between* the needs of labor *versus* the need for more capital expenditures.

(d) *In future years*, as you rerun those slides you'll relive the happy days *in retrospect*.

Most of the above, in one way or another, *say the same thing twice.* In (a) just say "in 1962 *as in* 1961." In (b) you could make it "The causes of this reaction *are* excess oxygen." But that sounds a little confusing, with its nonagreement in number between "are" and "oxygen," so perhaps a better way would be simply: "This reaction is caused by an excess of oxygen." In (c) make it: "between the needs of labor *and* the need for more capital expenditure." Example (d) says the *same* thing at the *end* of a sentence that was said at the *beginning* of it.

"These people realize they are in a *life-or-death* struggle for *survival.*" Survival *means* life-or-death.

PARTICIPIAL (vs. infinitive, or prepositional, form)—To many readers there is a subtle but appreciable difference, in certain situations, between using the participial form of a verb and the prepositional-phrase construction.
EXAMPLES:
He proposed to increase American imports as a means *to correct* the balance-of-payments situation.
. . . they wanted money to finance a broadened program *to sell* American goods in foreign markets.
In each of the above examples the objective sought is a continuing one, not a one-shot effort, and when this is the case, the participial form does a smoother job of conveying that feeling. As:
He proposed to increase American imports as a means of *correcting* the balance-of-payments situation.
. . . they wanted money to finance a broadened program *for selling* American goods in foreign markets.
In each of these particular examples the change to the -ing form serves to avoid having two consecutive "to" phrases, but that is just incidental.

Pretended Significance

LEAVE IT ALONE—"Use of special fasteners shaved man-hours 56 per cent in one packaging area alone." . . . A typical press agent subtlety is tossing in that word "alone." If the reference to saved man-hours had been strictly quantitative it would be all right, but when it is expressed in percentage the "alone" becomes pretentious and, to some degree, dishonest.

"In the record-breaking first quarter, 77,000 units were shipped. In March alone, 5,000 more units were shipped than in February."

Another example of the Pretended Significance ploy. The second sentence is intended to imply that there is great significance that in March (note the intensifier "alone") more units were shipped than in February. But February *is* one of the three months in the period we're talking about! So the comparison between March and February adds nothing, really, to the point that it was a good *quarter*.

Saying It Twice

"The *first* soft drink to use carbon dioxide instead of bicarbonate of soda is said to have been *originally* concocted in Tarboro, N.C. in 1894."

If it was the first one, and it was concocted at a given time, that must have been the original concocting, mustn't it?

"The *maximum daily* allowance is *not to exceed* $12 *per day*."
A *pair* of daily doubles there, in one short sentence.

"They increased the *age* of the straight whiskies in this blend
to 100 months *old*."

"Using a rough rule of thumb, we estimated that . . ."
A rule of thumb *is* rough; "estimated" also conveys the idea
of imprecision.

"In that *year,* fewer that 500,000 whatzits were being made
annually."
If you say *"in* that year" you have to say simply X whatzits
"were made." (If you were talking about a period covering
several years during which there was an average annual output
of X whatzits, start with "In those times" or "In that era.")

"The people who are opposing this legislation are *crying wolf
without cause*."
If the boy had cried wolf *with* cause that figure of speech
would never have been invented, would it?

". . . *no wonder* some managers are *understandably* skittish
about venturing into this *highly competitive no-man's land*."
If there's *no wonder* about it, it's *understandable,* is it not?
And when was the last time you saw a no-man's land, either in
war or peace, that was not highly competitive, to say the least?
. . . See how much sharper is: "no wonder some managers are
skittish about venturing into this no-man's land."

UNBELIEVABLE—"Mr. Goldstone believes the *reason for* the tremendous popularity of imports is *based on* two factors."
What are the two things wrong with this sentence? (1) Mr.
Goldstone *said he* believes (you don't know whether he really
believes it; you just know he said he believes it). (2) "The *rea-*

son for the tremendous popularity is *based on*" says the same thing twice! . . . The reason is not based on the factors. Say either, "The popularity is based on two factors," or "There are two reasons for the popularity."

"Mr. Jones said the *reason* for the brandy's success was *due to* its superior quality." . . . "With the *exception* of Abercrombie, all the *other* members of the team were in clean uniforms.

Series Business

An oft-encountered difficulty arises from a writer's failing to recognize when he has come to the end of a series. Here's a particularly elaborate example:

> The Danube has particular social, political and economic significance because it passes from West Germany and Austria in the free West through the Soviet satellite countries—Hungary, Yugoslavia, Czechoslovakia, Bulgaria, Rumania and the Soviet Union itself before emptying into the Black Sea.

What's wrong with it? The series of things identified as satellite countries does not include "the Soviet Union itself," quite obviously. So put "and" between Bulgaria and Rumania, and the second dash after Rumania.

UNRESOLVED SERIES—". . . thermometers are put to use to determine to what extent a new feature will save cooking time, fuel costs and preserve texture, color, flavor and nutrition in foods."

How do you "fuel" a cost?

But the sentence invited you to do that, because it invited

you to believe that this new feature will *do* three things—*save* cooking time, *fuel* costs, and *preserve*, etc.

It is the old problem of failing to realize that the third element in what appears to be a series is of a different nature than the first two and that therefore the series (of two) should be buttoned up before you go on to the third thing.

The solution is simple. Just put an "and" in place of that comma between "time" and "fuel," and put the comma after "costs."

Parallel, for illustrative purposes: Surely you would not write: "She used to date every Tom, Dick, Harry and helped Frank with his algebra."

You'd make it: "She used to date every Tom, Dick and Harry, and helped Frank with his algebra."

INCOMPLETED SERIES—Does it bother you to hear (most) football broadcasters declaring that such-and-such a play was an "incomplete*d*" forward pass? Probably not, judging from the

ceaseless flow of "incompleted"-series sentences across this desk.
EXAMPLE:
Overnutrition can cause irritability, skin disorders, kidney and
  stomach ailments.

What's wrong with it? Well, it reads as though "kidney" were
the name of a disease. Note that irritability is one thing, skin
disorders is the second, and ailments (of either kidney or stomach) is the third thing in that series. So of course that whole
third thing should be preceded by an "and."

A few more oversimplified examples:
The soldier was ragged, unshaven, and walked with a proud
  step.
The grocer made a profit on apples, peaches but lost on ruta-
  baga.
I got good grades in history, arithmetic, and was popular with
  the teacher.
The tractor could plow, harrow and cost less than a hired man.

Singular

Singularly more effective in almost every case where you are
writing about "people" of almost any kind—housewives, hus-
bands, pilots, motorists, etc.—is the tactic of telling it in the
singular instead of in the *plural*. It makes your sentence easier
to write, you're less likely to get into clumsy problems of
agreement in number between subject and verb, and, most important, your point has more impact because the reader more
readily *identifies himself* in the role you're talking about.

Spelling Clue

Not everyone can be a natural-born good speller. But anyone can spell somewhat better if he keeps mindful of the way many words "grow"—especially the longer ones—and pays attention to the often-obvious matter of *why* a word means what it does.

For example, the other day a man wrote that something was "a temporary *abberation*."

Now if you know, even in a vague way, what "aberration" means (and know that it has nothing to do with the measuring out of food supplies in a monastery) it would be next to impossible for you to go so far astray—that is, to be so *ab errant* —as to spell it *abbe-ration*.

Stumble Puns

"I believe it is possible to build a safer car than we now have on the highways. Steps are being taken in that direction and undoubtedly will be *accelerated* in the next few years" (italics added).

When you do stumble into one like that—and realize you have done so—it's a good idea to review the situation judicially and make up your mind whether you want to let it ride. Generally, unless it's a pun you *mean* to make, and one that really helps make your point, it will be wiser to choose another word. If you're *that* subtle about it (as in the example above) many a reader will probably feel that he (the reader) has spotted something that the writer himself wasn't even aware of.

Here's a beaut of a pun-within-a-pun from a metropolitan paper. It is surely not an unconscious one, but has the earmarks of having just come along in the normal course of a sentence. The writer made the most of it—and in the process gave posterity a neat example of a truly constructive use of the much-misused "literally" (the story was a backgrounder on a gambling-swindling case):

However, the case against them literally went *out the window* when Abe Reles, the memorable canary who could *sing* but not *fly,* somehow fell to his death from a guarded room in the Half Moon Hotel in Coney Island before he could testify.

Excerpt from a memo on press-relations policies for a hospital: ". . . except in case of sexual assault, when no statement may be made as to who is responsible for the incident. Refer these *queeries* to the police."

"But *lines* of authority became *tangled* during his one-man *rein,* and . . ."

Accidental or not? The word was *reign,* of course, and it still would have been a pun if spelled correctly, but not a very good one.

". . . an ambidextrous pair of scissors that, it is estimated, cuts by 75 per cent the time it would take with an ordinary pair."

Resist that impulse.

". . . thereafter the jeweler, at very little cost to himself, continues to furnish batteries *without charge,* as part of his guarantee."

Any fee at all for furnishing that kind of batteries would be excessive, wouldn't it?

In a story urging everyone to dispose properly of Christmas wrappings, decorations, trees, etc. (so that "the glitter won't turn to litter"), the typist typed, quite innocently: "4. Don't dump old *Christmess* trees and wreaths in the back yard, street or vacant lot" (italics added).

That's a good example of a stumble pun that, once detected, should be rejected—on grounds of taste.

". . . and the materials are known by the polysyllabic names of polyurethanes and polyamide prepolymers."

Why not let the reader discover for himself that polyurethanes and polyamide prepolymers are many-syllabled words? He can do it. The above-quoted construction indicates that the writer of the sentence wished to show that he knew a polysyllabic synonym, himself, for "long word." (Actually, there was an opportunity for a sly aside there, in the fact that all three of the exotic words are literally *poly*syllabic in two ways, but the straight-faced way in which the sentence was written did not indicate there was any kind of pun intended.)

One of our boys swears he saw it with his own eyes, a headline in a New Jersey paper about a basketball game between a couple of Catholic high schools: GUARDIAN ANGEL STOPS CONCEPTION.

Syllabization—End-of-the-Line

This is a group with which one is glad to be id-
    entified.

The above illustrates (being a violation of) a principle of
syllabization with which all writers—and certainly copyists and
typesetters—should be familiar, namely that *pronunciation* plays
a decisive part in deciding how words should be divided.

In the quoted sentence, for example, the "id" syllable invites
the reader to deduce that this is the start of a word that starts
with a short-*i* sound; then he has to shift gears mentally when
he gets to the start of the next line and finds the word was "i-
dentified."

If the word had been "ideology," either division, "i" or "id,"
would have been defensible. Why? Because that word may be
pronounced either *i-deology* or *id-eology.*

Practically, it is neither necessary nor desirable to divide a
word, at all, at the end of a line if you are going to be able to
get only one lonesome letter out there. Nobody needs to save
space that badly. A couple more examples:

Almost all high schools in this country have chemical *lab-
    oratories* with . . .

BUT

On the southern outskirts of London there is a large *la-
    boratory* where experiments in . . . [because the British
    pronounce the word la-*bor*-atree].

One person may *pre-fer* steak, while another expresses a *pref-
    erence* for fish.

Pro-duce, but *prod-uct* . . . *de-cayed,* but *dec-ade* . . .

The group sang songs of *pro-test* in front of the *Prot-estant*
    church.

To Quote or Not

Here's a critical quote on quotes, from the Kansas City *Star's* stylebook: "The excessive use of quotes in headlines and around words and phrases that do not represent direct quotation indicates vagueness and smallness of vocabulary. . . . Find the right word and serve it up without apology."

An embarrassing instance of overuse of quotes was the gratuitous placing, by an editor, of quotation marks around the middle name of the late Smith Wildman Brookhart, senator from Iowa. It was, as some may remember, his real middle name.

NICKNAMES need not be quoted when used parenthetically along with the person's name, as in Edward (Whitey) Ford, except when the nickname is an unusual or epithetic one, as John W. ("Bet A Million") Gates or Frank ("The Enforcer") Nitti.

Avoid making a point of an obvious and routine nickname: "William T. (known to his friends as 'Bill') Logan has announced his candidacy."

QUOTING VERBATIM?—In a sports column praising a baseball player of many seasons ago—and with no indication that he was a backwoods or hillbilly type—the columnist quoted the athlete as saying: "If the shoulder hadn't healed properly I *would of* come back to the big leagues as a left-handed thrower."

The general journalistic rule is that, unless you are trying to make a point that will be made more effectively by quoting verbatim a comment in which the grammar is slightly non-standard (e.g., fight manager Yussel Jacobs' classic "he should of stood in bed"; the Dizzy Dean commentary, "he slud into third base"; the protest of a boxer saved from first-round annihilation by the referee, "They should of left it went"), you should cast quotes in reasonably correct grammar. In this particular case that *would've* been especially easy to do.

STILL VULNERABLE—Putting an uncomplimentary epithet in quotation marks neither (a) softens the unfavorable reference nor (b) relieves the writer of the onus of having made that reference himself, when the source of the quoted words or words is not apparent.

EXAMPLE:

. . . a civil rights group formed here about three years ago with assistance from Ronald Rogers, the Omaha-based community organizer and "professional radical."

Far from softening or disclaiming the epithet, the quotes simply call it more forcefully to any reader's attention.

Unanswered Questions

"The Soandso Company will break ground for a new multistory building at Twelfth and Elm Streets."

Multistory indeed! Is the company breaking ground for this building without having decided how many stories tall it's going to be? Of course not. It knows, but for some reason—legal or otherwise—does not wish to say. So why arouse curiosity, not to mention cynicism, by throwing in that word "multistory," thus raising a question that you do not wish to answer? Just say "for an office building. . . ." (If they're breaking ground for it, it cannot be an *old* building, can it?)

Verbalization

AN INVENTION that does not seem to have been mothered by Necessity (or by any mother, for that matter): "When confronted with this, she protested that, instead, she *reverenced* Hemingway." This is from a literary column in the same city whence Paul Revere departed on his celebrated ride . . . can it be that even there plain "revered" is no longer good enough?

"The new warehouse was custom-architected for the trade." That's our nomination for the farthest-out verbalization of a noun since the one where the Madison Avenue doll, talking about the number and variety of chores to be taken care of in connection with a certain TV broadcast, wound up with: "and besides there were all those sponsors' sales representatives to be *liaised.*"

MOST FASCINATING VERBALIZATION OF ANY WORLD SERIES: Yogi Berra, explaining what happened to the dipping liner that went through him for a three-base error: "I guess I must have *nonchalanted* it."

Verbal Noun

THE APT APOSTROPHE—Even some quite literate persons frequently ask why a copy desk converts a word into the possessive case in certain locutions involving the combining of a noun (like "city") with a verb indicating some action it might take (like "operating"). For example, "There are certain advantages in a city's operating its own garbage disposal system."

If this puzzles you, maybe the following will help: "The boss frowned upon *me* looking out the window." Which one was looking out the window? "The boss frowned upon *my* looking out the window." No ambiguity here; the boss was disapproving someone's (my) looking out the window. He did not frown *at me* while either of us looked out the window. In fact, he did not frown *at me* at any time. And he did not frown at the mere act of looking out the window as it might be practiced by someone else (not working here).

But, Boy! he did definitely frown at *my* looking out that window!

Wobbly Words

'TO MY KNOWLEDGE' is an untrustworthy and weasily ambiguous phrase. The reader never can be sure whether the speaker is genuinely being emphatic about his knowledge of a fact or is leaving himself an "out" in case he later finds it expedient to deny having made a positive assertion.

OFTEN UNNECESSARY are the words "presently" and "currently." If you are saying that a laboratory *is* being built, or a campaign *is* being organized, or an executive *is* on the high seas returning from an ocean cruise, there is no need for either of those words. It is especially desirable to minimize—better still, avoid—the use of "presently" when you mean "at present," because the primary meaning of "presently" is *not* "at present," but "*soon.*"

THREE FOR THE L-O-O-K I-T U-P DEPT.

It's a good idea to have the product available in a *plethora* of sizes.

This will enable us to earn *fulsome* credit from the industry.

"The logic of this position is so clear that I will not *belabor* it further," Prof. Emerson said.

ADVERBOSIS—"In the last few years our company has become much more technologically oriented."

Nope. Make it "technology-oriented," if you have to say it that way.

Why? The company is oriented toward a *thing*; i.e., a *noun*; i.e., technology. It is not oriented "in a technological *manner*."

ADVERBOSITY?

"Jimmy Valentine" was the hero of an oft-played melodrama of a couple of generations ago, a crook with the ability to open combination-locked safes without benefit of dynamite, because of the superhuman sensitivity of his finger tips. (He felt, and listened to, the tumblers fall into place as he fiddled with the combination.)

So it could be said that he was the world-champion safe-cracker because he felt so expertly . . . i.e., he felt well.

But one day he felt *badly*. As a result, he failed to open the safe.

And he felt bad about it.

The foregoing fable is designed to illuminate the point that to say or write, "I felt badly" (about failing to meet Margie at the airport, for instance; or about getting a D-minus in English), is to indulge in language that is not only overelegant but incorrect.

To illuminate it a bit further:

In most situations where this expression comes up, the person using it is confessing that he felt embarrassed, or chagrined, or frustrated, or ashamed, or disappointed. Something like that. But would you ever use the adverbial form of any of those? Of course not. So there is no reason to tack the "ly" onto "bad." If this booklet succeeds in putting over this point, the author will feel goodly about it.

"The decision has already been made, but pain-staking study will still be necessary," etc. Maybe Bartlett's had it wrong, and it should have been: "Genius is an infinite capacity for staking pain."

"In the realignment of executive positions, Vice President Forrest will become the *overall* head." . . . Previously he was *underwear* supervisor, or something?

> Overall and underway! . . .
> Hardly ever comes a day
> When all our guys and gals are on the ball
> In spelling under way and over-all.
>
> With our ballpoint we have flailed,
> And for years and years have railed,
> But folks disdain that simple hy-phen-ation,
> And, what is even simpler, sep a ra tion.
>
> So we'll put it into rhyme
> (For the umpty-thousandth time)
> That overalls are clothes that workers work in,
> While underways are tunnels lurkers lurk in!

BE SAFE as well as SECURE: Let's keep in mind the distinction between "obtain," "procure" and "get," on the one hand, and "secure," on the other. A story accenting the expensiveness of some marine equipment required for a given job said the contractor acquired three barges of one type, another barge of another type, and a certain type of dragline. Then the next sentence quoted the contractor as saying: "But *securing* the equipment was only a part of the project." Which could sound as though he were talking about the importance of making sure his barges didn't drift away. What he was talking about was the way in which they were *obtained,* i.e., financed.

A mid-Atlantic state is a wet state . . . because it's in the middle of the Atlantic ocean. If you're referring to one of the group comprising New York, Pennsylvania and New Jersey, you have to spell it Middle Atlantic state.

'WITH' and 'TO'—Avoid opening stories with "With . . ." It is a weak and punchless word. Try to use one that grabs hold of the reader with more vigor. Besides, the "With . . ." opening technique is timeworn and readily recognized as characteristic of publicity copy.

One device present-day newswriters often use to help them string two thoughts together quickly and tightly is that of tacking on an infinitive clause using the preposition "to." Occasionally it backfires because of the connotation of "intent" that is inherent in the word "to." As in this specimen, in a dispatch about a man who telephoned the police about a blonde who had been found shot to death:

Police tried to detain him on the telephone, but he replied he "didn't want to get mixed up in this affair." Before he hung up he told police he had been out with Mrs. Carl several times and had called at her apartment last night to find her dead.

Well, then, he shouldn't have been surprised. She was.

INAPPROPRIATE: ". . . several significant medical discoveries were made during the year, discoveries that lead *inexorably* to longer, healthier lives." . . . *Inexorable* is not the word to use in referring to something *favorable* that's going to happen, no matter how certain it is (especially some good thing that is related to your client's good works) because *inexorable* applies to something that happens, or is going to happen, in spite of its being entreated against, literally "prayed against." Why not say, in simple Anglo-Saxon, "discoveries that are bound to bring longer, healthier lives."

Similarly, you wouldn't write that Junior practiced his piano lessons "relentlessly" unless you were actually (and facetiously) making the point that he had a sadistic attitude and his practicing constituted a definitely torturous experience for the instrument itself or for harassed ear-witnesses. Say, rather: "faithfully," "religiously," "assiduously," "doggedly," "dutifully," etc. In short, use the word that says what you mean.

OVERUSE of "good, strong, favorable" words (that is, the failure to resist the temptation to throw 'em all in) sometimes backfires. Note this amusing example: "The Suchandsuch manufacturer told the audience his company is one of many *contributing directly* to the *growing need* for greater reliability." What he meant to say was that his company was helping *meet* that need, not contributing to it.

A POINT TO BE LABORED—"Belabor" is fast challenging "comprise" as the most-often-misapplied word in the American language. When one needlessly or tiresomely presses a point of argument or explanation he is *laboring* it. To *belabor* is to beat, hit, or whip, in a physical sense. True, a second meaning is "to beat with words; attack verbally," but that still is not what someone is referring to when he politely murmurs, "Well, I don't want to *belabor* the point, but—"

FAD WORDS: "Something needs to be done, they contend, to *beef up* the *expertise* of our foreign-service personnel."

Let's beware of beefing-up everything, especially where the strengthening—as is the case here—so pointedly relates to mental rather than physical strength. After all, even the strongest beeves are not distinguished for their *expertise,* are they?

A PLUS WE SHOULD BE MINUS—"The increasing desire to go home, *plus* widespread disagreement over Administration proposals, *have combined* to make things uncertain." . . . It is redundant to use "plus" in this kind of sentence. You don't say, "A *plus* B have combined to make a good doubles team"; you just say, "A *and* B have combined to make a good doubles team." Or else: "A plus B makes a good doubles team." All clear? . . . (Even so, they'd still probably lose to the Australians.)

". . . because of the corrosion, pipes were having to be replaced at intervals averaging only three months apart."
Strike the *apart.* The *intervals* were *not* three months *apart.*

"If Junior frequently leads his Cub Scout friends to the cookie jar in the pantry, the wear and tear can *reap* havoc."
Let's make it *wreak,* shall we, in the classic phrase? Junior's the one who might reap something—like a swat in the pants.

"All these factors," Jones said, "make any strict rule-of-thumb impossible."
This is a contradiction in terms: A strict rule is one thing; a rule-of-thumb is almost a direct opposite. For the most part, people use figurative words or phrases in order to gain impact or clarity. So when you use a figurative term, be sure you know what it means.

"This is one example of the often hidden pitfalls in that business."
Whaddaya mean, often hidden? Being hidden is what makes a pitfall a pitfall.

". . . the impact of such things as the civil rights movement and consumer *preoccupation* with service and quality."

Make it "the consumer's *intensifying concern* with service and quality."

"Preoccupation" does not mean *consciously* more occupied with one thing than with anything else; it means occupied with something other than the matter at hand.

"This was another illustration of the *relentless* push of the industry toward more efficient production."

Better than "relentless" would be "unremitting," "ceaseless" or "tireless." Why? Because "relentless" has the strong connotation of showing no mercy, no let-up in pursuit of something hurtful or punitive.

"The animated sign will tell its story in a series of eight sequences."

Probably not. It's probably *one sequence* of eight *scenes*.

"Or where can a guy find relief from all those *hair shirt* tasks around the house that only a wife can dream up?"

"Hair shirt" carries definitely and solely the idea of *self-imposed penance* (from the monks' mortification); it is not something thrown at you by someone else. Even a wife.

BRING and TAKE—This happens much more often in conversation than in written material, but there does seem to be widespread lack of appreciation of the distinct difference between "bring" and "take." Maybe these examples will help:

Bring back, bring back, oh, bring back my Bonnie to me.

VERSUS

You Can't Bring It With You.

Of course the verb in the George S. Kaufman play's title was *Take*. It had to be: only somebody in Heaven, or the Other Place, would be grammatically correct in using "bring" in that context.

A musical mnemonic: Contrast "Bringing in the Sheaves" with the title of a slightly less reverent song: *"Take* Back Your Mink!"

INCLUDE IT OUT, PLEASE: "The six industries include aircraft, automobiles, electrical machinery, machine tools, railroads and steel."

That *is* six!

One should use the word "include" in such a context only when listing only some—not all—of the items embodied in a given grouping.

PRE-DICT EDICT—"Space programs have spawned entirely new concepts in reliability, and the ocean will present an even greater challenge," he predicted.

Now, wait. The first of the two things the man said was in the past perfect tense; therefore he could not *predict* that, he simply *said* it. The second part could properly be described as a prediction. So make it: "He pointed out that space programs have spawned entirely new concepts in reliability, and predicted that the ocean will present an even greater challenge."

SAY IT! Do not be afraid to use "said" repeatedly. It's much better than reaching for presumed synonyms like "asserted," "stated," "declared." . . . However, this is not to discourage the intelligent use of variants that convey desirable, specific overtones of meaning—like "explained," "warned," "urged," "reported," "acknowledged," "demanded," "emphasized."

SIC TRANSITIVE—"Its development *culminated* a three-year, multimillion-dollar research program." A popular error, but nevertheless an error. "Culminate" is an *intransitive* verb only. That means that *something* can *culminate* (usually with the preposition "in"), but you cannot *culminate* something.

A couple of Ripples from Elsewhere: Beautiful actress being

interviewed on TV: "Well, the chief reason for my success is that I have been in this line of work since I was 14 years of age and I have a *dearth* of experience." . . . Governor of a "great state" (aren't they all?) commenting on the school-prayer issue: "Yes, ah'll repeat it; ah said that the Court has *usurpated* its authority." . . . And in a skull session not too far from here: "Well, of course, this is only a *hunchback* opinion, but—"

AX ME ANOTHER—"You will note that this version *hues* pretty close to the official line."
The color line?

FINE POINT: "Rural homeowners now have a greater opportunity of *securing* home improvement loans."
Discriminating writers would do well to bear in mind the difference between "secure" and "obtain." There is particular reason for being mindful of this in a sentence about loans, because the obtaining of a loan (getting somebody to lend you something) can be quite different from the securing of a loan (putting up adequate collateral, or security, so the lender can feel secure). As it happens, "obtaining" would have been the correct word in the sentence quoted.
Another example (because of another meaning): "Hearing Watkins' cries for help coming from the middle of the lake, the lifeguard *secured* a boat and went to the rescue."
If he secured the boat and then went to Watkins' aid he must have done the rescuing on sheer swim-power. . . . What he actually did to the boat was obtain, or get, or grab, or hop into.

UNCONSCIOUS NEOLOGISM (politician on TV)— ". . . and if we follow the platform of our opponents it can only lead to more and more *mediocracy*."

'RANGING FROM'—Too often the expression "ranging from" is applied to pairs (or more) of things that actually "range" from about E to F—instead of from A to Z, or at least C to W, which is what the "ranging from" locution implies.

WRONG WORD: "North Dakota's Blue Cross has announced the installation of an electronic computer which it *estimates* will *significantly reduce* operating costs."

It is not correct to say "estimates" unless you are referring to at least some degree of *measurement,* such as 10 per cent, or "nearly a third," or something like that.

PASSÉ TENSE—"As far back as 1958 there were 230 varieties, and the number now, he *predicted,* probably *has* doubled or tripled."

You cannot possibly predict something that already has to be referred to in the past or past perfect tense.

OLD-FASHIONED, SPACE-WASTING: "The exhibit should *be inclusive of* samples of. . . ." What's wrong with simply "should include"?

"Never before has the dental profession *been possessed of* so many effective weapons for prevention of tooth decay." Why not simply "had"? Or, if you feel a need for building it up, "had access to," or "had at its disposal."

CAPITAL OFFENSE—"Jones is a graduate of Yale University and a former Naval officer."

He is either a former Navy officer (if it was the U.S. Navy) or a former naval officer. (You could, however, refer to him as having graduated from the Naval Academy—provided he had done so, and provided it was the U.S. one.)

IMPORTANT: BEWARE IMPORTANTLY—The late John Lardner had a piece a few years ago in *Newsweek* on what he called "misplaced grammatical snobbishness," chiefly attacking the tendency to write: "And, more important*ly,* . . ."

An excerpt or two: "Thus a noted radio-TV reviewer writes 'She has nice teeth and, more importantly, she sings on key.' For a singer to sing on key importantly she would have to ride up to the microphone on a white horse and be introduced by the Mayor or the Secretary of State. . . . 'He has learned the strike zone,' writes a baseball critic, 'and, more importantly, he is hitting the ball for distance.' Hitting the ball importantly calls for certain props. You visualize the batsman coming to the plate with all his war medals pinned to his chest, and swinging the bat to the music of a brass band playing 'Hail To The Chief'." Lardner then imagined what the home dinner-table conversation of such an adverbalizer might be, guessing that the man might say to his moppet: "If you don't like your spinach, well, finely and dandily, don't eat it." And he further guesses that the said moppet would thereupon go out to play hide-and-seek and, being "it" and having counted to 20, would holler: "Readily or not, here I come!"

Speaking of UNNEEDED LY's, here's a striking example:

"Steer a course between the channel buoys or markers. The red, *evenly* numbered buoys should be on your right . . ."

And, more importantly, if you don't steer it that way, the evenly tempered skipper will be illy disposed to look kindlyly upon it!

VI.

Words to Watch Out For

Often misspelled . . . often misused . . . often confused with another word. These are the things that happen to these "words to watch out for."

abrogate—to annul, repeal
arrogate—to usurp; claim or take without right

absentee, absenteeism—be mindful of the strong implication of *deliberate* or *habitual* absenting, especially in the "ism" form

abstruse—hard to understand; complicated
obtuse—dull; opposite of *acute*

accommodate—two c's, two m's

adduce—to cite; bring forward as evidence or argument
educe—to draw forth; elicit; evoke

adverse—acting against; unfavorable; unpropitious
averse—unwilling; reluctant

abjure—to renounce; forswear; recant
adjure—to command or entreat solemnly

adviser—(not advisor)

*affect and effect (example 1)—"Sunshine affects people in different ways; its effect is beneficial to most."
affect and effect (example 2)—"If he didn't affect such a nasty manner, he would have a better chance of effecting a compromise."
affect and effect (example 3)—"The troops were not affected by the strafing, but pushed ahead and effected a landing."

airplane—not "aeroplane"

allotment—two *l*'s, one *t*

allusion—an indirect reference
illusion—a false appearance
elusion—act of eluding or evading

alumna—female graduate (plural, alumnae)
alumnus—male graduate (plural, alumni)
alumni—collective plural when both genders are included

amiable—friendly in sense of genial, good-humored, pleasant, outgoing
amicable—friendly as distinct from hostile: "amicable discussion" (in situation where some unfriendliness might have been expected)

anxious—be careful about using this word where you may mean *eager*

apace—it does not mean "in step with" or "abreast"; it means *swiftly*, i.e., *at a fast pace*

appraise—to set a value on, rate
apprise—to inform, advise, make known

---

* See also page 81.

assay—to test, analyze critically
essay—to attempt; also, a treatise

attendee—no such word

ax—(not axe)

balance—do not use when you mean the rest or the remainder
(unless you mean an actual mathematical balance)

belabor—to wallop, beat, drub; to assail verbally. Except
in some of the more permissive of the most recent dictionaries, this word is not synonymous with, or an intensifier of, "labor" in its sense of tiresomely and unnecessarily
arguing or explaining. Thus the phrase "I don't wish to
belabor the point" entails an unnecessary syllable.

believe—you do not know what Senator Soaper believes,
you know only what he *said* he believes

bellwether—two *l*'s, no *a*; if you misspell this you make it
obvious you don't understand why you're using it!

benchmark—fad word in role of alternative to hallmark, as bespeaking quality; actually it has a specific meaning related to sea-level or tidal *measurements,* and there is no appropriateness in using it as a mark of *quality.*

benefit, benefiting—single *t*; note also combating, worshiper, et al.

bird's-eye view—note spelling and division

blond—noun, masculine
blonde—noun, feminine
blond—adjective, regardless of gender

breakthrough—a great word when it first broke through; now it's weak from overwork

bring and take—you bring something from elsewhere to here; you take something from here to elsewhere

broadcast—past tense (not broadcasted)

brunet, brunette, brunet—same procedure as for blond, blonde, etc.

brussels sprouts—lower-case

buses—plural of bus (vehicle) . . . (busses are lusty kisses)

calendar—record of days, weeks, months, etc.
calender—a basic machine of the rubber, textile and other industries
colander—a sieve
Callander—birthplace (Ontario) of the Dionne quintuplets

caliber—not "calibre" . . . center, theater, fiber likewise

callous—the adjective: hardened, as skin
callus—the noun: hardened, thickened skin
callow—unfledged; young and inexperienced

cancel, canceled, canceling

canvas—coarse cloth used for tents, etc.
canvass—to solicit systematically

capital—principal city; also, of course, funds, etc.
capitol—refers only to actual building where a state legislature or the U.S. Congress (capital *C* in that case) meets

catalog—not catalogue

category—not cata-

center—preferred style is *er* in this word and in others, such as fiber, luster, specter, theater (but it *is* Rockville Centre, N.Y., and Centre College, at Danville, Ky.)

chaperon—not chaperone

cigarette—not cigaret

climactic—pertaining to a climax
climatic—pertaining to climate

complacent—smug, self-satisfied
complaisant—obliging, amenable

complected—do not use when you mean complexioned

complement—to go well with, augment, round out (akin to *complete*)
compliment—to say something nice about: "the First Lady acknowledged *compliments* on the way the new spinet *complemented* the French Room decor."

comprise—unquestionably the most frequently misused word in the language
comprise (example 1)—"The secretaries of the State, Defense, Interior and other departments COMPOSE the Cabinet" (that is, they constitute it).
comprise (example 2)—"The cabinet COMPRISES the secretaries of the State, Defense . . . " (that is, it includes, embraces, contains them).

connive—(from the Latin for "wink at")—assent to a wrong
by pretending not to know of it
contrive—to devise, improvise; to scheme or plot

consensus—not "concensus" (it's akin to assent, consent, dis-
sent, etc.); avoid writing "the consensus of opinion"

consistently—not always a satisfactory synonym for "regularly" or "steadily"

continual—in steady, but not unbroken succession; recurring
regularly
continuous—without even momentary interruption

controlled, controlling—double *l* (accent falls on that syllable); see jeweler, leveled, traveled

consul—commercial representative of a country
consular—of or pertaining to the above
council—governing or deliberative group
councilor—member of the above
counsel—advice; advise; one who advises
counselor—one who counsels

credible—believable
creditable—deserving credit, worthy
credulous—easily believing, naïve

data—this is a plural word, but do not feel you have to use
a plural verb with it if the resulting phrase sounds pro-
fessorial or stuffy, which is quite likely

decry—to cry down; censure loudly
descry—to discover with the eye, especially from afar; to
detect

deprecate—to plead against, disapprove, view with regret
depreciate—to undervalue; to fall in value; to speak slight-
ingly of

diesel—lower-case *d*

different from—do not write "different than"

diffident—not synonymous with indifferent or aloof; it means shy, retiring, lacking in self-assertiveness (cf. *con*fident)

dilemma—not a good synonym for "problem" unless you mean a problem of choosing between two (di) alternatives, neither of which is very promising

discomfiture—defeat, frustration (has nothing to do with discomfort)

disinterested—impartial, unbiased
uninterested—not interested, unconcerned

dived—this is the past tense of "dive"; "dove" is archaic or colloquial, but in some instances it may sound better than "dived"

divers—various, sundry, assorted
diverse—contrasting, opposite

drought—preferable to drouth
dutch oven—lower-case *d*

eleemosynary—a slippery one, but not because of any *eels* in it

employe—our style (because it's that of AP and NY *Times*)

ended, ending—say "for the nine months end*ed*" when the period *has* ended; use "end*ing*" in such phrases when the date given is in the future

enormity—be careful; enormousness is only its number 3 definition

equable—of uniform condition; steady, not easily disturbed; i.e., equable climate, equable disposition
equitable—fair, impartial, characterized by justice

equally—remember not to tack on "as" after this word; equally means "as much as" (say something like "fully as" if you have to)

etc.—not desirable; a preferable phrase is "and so forth"

euphemism—a word or expression less unpleasant or blunt than the more accurate term would be
euphuism—an instance of high-flown, affected style in speech or writing

fallible—capable of being wrong
fallacious—mistaken; unsoundly reasoned

farther—use in referring to actual distance or time
further—use in figurative references: "Nothing could be further from my thought."

fewer—preferable to *less* when discrete numbers are involved

fiberglass—preferred as the generic term; Fiberglas is the trade name

firstly—do not start an enumeration with this; it's old-fashioned and leads to complications. "First" is better.

flaunt—to display ostentatiously, gaudily, impudently or even (but not necessarily) defiantly: "The typical teen-ager *flaunts* his sartorial and tonsorial unconventionality."
flout—to show contempt or disregard for: "Engstrom *flouted* the Scoutmaster's warnings and set out across the rubbery ice."

flyer—preferable to flier

focus, focused, focusing

forceful—strong, emphatic
forcible—attained or accomplished by physical force

fortuitous—only the most recent and "language growth"—

minded dictionaries ascribe to this the meaning of *favorable* chance, not *mere* chance (and then only secondarily)

front runner—see *pinch hitter*

fulsome—does not mean "generous," "abundant,'" "bounteous," etc.; it means "offensively excessive," "insincere"

gauge—not guage

glamour—the "our" spelling seems preferred by most papers, possibly because of subconscious analogy to "l'amour," whereas, conversely, the "or" ending has the less-pleasant association with "clamor"
glamorous—considerations used in above do not apply to this form

graduated—don't be afraid to say Soandso graduated. It's no longer required to say "was graduated" every time.

gray—(*grey* is British)

healthful—conducive to good health; wholesome
healthy—in good health; strong, robust

height—not heighth or heigth

helicopter—pronounce it with a short *e*, because it relates to helix, a spiral (cf. helicon, helical, etc.), whereas long *e* sound is used in words stemming from "helios," the sun (cf. heliotrope, heliograph, etc.)

hopefully—beware of using this in a way that imputes the emotion of hoping to an inanimate object: "Hopefully the bus will arrive on time."

imply—to hint, denote or intimate ("his frown implied deep irritation")

infer—to deduce or conclude ("from his frown I inferred that he was deeply irritated"). Let's preserve the distinction between these words even though one new dictionary gives "hint, imply" as *the number 3 definition* of infer!

importantly—an unnecessary and illogical adverbial form in such expressions as: "My new secretary will be fine when she lengthens her skirt and, more important*ly*, learns to spell."

indispensable—not "ible"

ingenious—clever, skillful, inventive
ingenuous—naïve, frank, artless

inimical—hostile, unfriendly; not synonymous with "inimitable"

iniquity—sin
inequity—unfairness, injustice

irregardless—an obvious double negative; illiterate (except when used with jocular intent). This in spite of some recent dictionaries.

jeweler—one *l* (likewise in traveler, other such words; use double *l* only in words where accent falls on that syllable)

knot—in nautical usage, a measure of speed, not of distance ("the ship was making 14 knots" means that it was traveling 14 nautical miles per hour). So do not write "14 knots an hour."

led—the correct past tense of the verb "to lead"

less—try to remember to write "fewer" when that's the more accurate word

matériel—French for "material." Use this spelling only where situation clearly requires it, and never write "war matériel."

meretricious—no relation whatever to "meritorious" (look it up and you'll see why)

minuscule—*you* can spell it right!

mitigate, militate—be sure you know which one's the one you mean

money—plural, moneys

mucous—the adjective
mucus—the noun

mural—please don't write anything about a "wall mural" (or an "egg omelet")

nevertheless—in spite of, even so, regardless of, still
none the less—writing these three words together does *not* create a word that is synonymous with nevertheless; most dictionaries do not even admit it as one word

newspaperman—(all one word)

niece—(spelled same as piece)

obsolescence—condition of *becoming* obsolete
obsoleteness—condition of *being* obsolete

odds-on—see *pinch hitter*

optimum—not necessarily better than "maximum"; in fact, less strong than "maximum"

ordinance—a local law; a statute
ordnance—military supplies; chiefly, but not exclusively, artillery

over—"more than" is preferred by most newspapers
over-age—too old; superannuated
overage—amount by which some quantity is too much; surplus

palate—roof of mouth; taste
pallet—low, portable platform
palette—artist's board

paris green—lower-case *p*

pendant—a hanging ornament
pendent—hanging (the participle)

penurious—not simply poor; stingy

permissible—not -able

phosphorous—the adjective
phosphorus—the noun

physiotherapy—all one word

pinch hitter—one of three sports terms used often outside of sports-page context, in figurative references. It is good for writers and editors to be aware that:

A *pinch hitter* is not merely one who substitutes for another, but one who is given a difficult assignment in a difficult situation where a timely and effective performance is needed, and he is one who, in the circumstances of his appearance, is *expected to do better than the one for whom he is batting.*

A *front runner* is, in true sports parlance, not merely a horse or a foot runner who happens to be "in front" at the time of writing (the way this term is so often used of political aspirants) but a competitor who tends to perform well while in front, or in the early stages of a race, but has something of a history of not doing so well when the contest comes (in another sports-page cliché) "down to the wire."

Odds-on is not a valid term to use in accenting the fact that one team, or one contestant, is heavily favored in a contest with only one other entrant. It is valid, and should be used, only to describe a situation where one entry (say a horse) is so outstanding that even though a considerable number of others are running, a bettor has to *give* odds to bet on this one against the whole field. So in a man-to-man or team-to-team contest "odds-on" is meaningless.

pinpoint—beware overuse

pipeline—all one word when referring to cross-country line; also in figurative use. Lines of pipe in a building, or even in city streets, are not pipelines.

Pittsburgh, Pa.—but Pittsburg, Kas.

plethora—it means more than just "plenty of"; it means excessive fullness, superfluity

podium—be careful not to use this when you mean "lectern" or "stage," or "rostrum"

postwar—no hyphen

precede, proceed, procedure—note spellings

precipitate—rash, headlong
precipitous—steep

premature—never say or write "too premature" (an obvious redundancy)

prescribe—to lay down as a rule, or regimen
proscribe—to denounce, condemn, ban

presently—if you mean "at present" it is better to write it that way, because "presently" primarily means "soon" or "before long"

principal—chief, head, leading
principle—doctrine, theory, basic rule, moral ideal

programming, programmed—two *m*'s

promise—as a verb, refers strictly to something *in the future*

prone—you can't lie prone on your back; *that's supine* (mnemonic: on your spine)

propeller—(not propellor)

proved—(preferable to proven, but not mandatory)

provided—do not use provid*ing* in the sense of "on condition that"

provident—thrifty, prudent, foresighted
providential—effected by divine intervention; fortunate

pushbutton—all one word

radioisotope—all one word

refurbish—"furbish" and "furnish" do not mean the same thing; therefore "refurbish" does not mean the same thing as "refurnish." If you are writing for perceptive readers, beware of using "refurbish" as though it embodied the idea of supplying new carpets, lamps, chairs, etc., *in addition* to making the place bright and clean by rubbing

salable, serviceable, sizable—note spellings

sanitarium OR sanatorium—but neither "sanitorium" nor "sanatarium"

secondly—leave off that "ly" (otherwise, to be consistent, you'd have to go back and make first firstly—and you might have thirdlies, fourthlies, etc. Who needs it?)

secure—much more than a mere synonym for "obtain" or "get"; indeed, can be misleading when used as such

serviceman—all one word

siege, sieve, seize—note positions of *i* and *e* in these words

simulate—assume the character or semblance of; imitate
stimulate—rouse to activity; goad

size, sized (in compounds)—most of the time the *d* is unnecessary, as in "king-size"; sometimes the whole "size"
is unnecessary, as, perhaps, in "large-size," and as, certainly, in "giant-size" (what is the distinguishing thing
about a giant, anyway?)

strata—a plural word; see caution under "data"

supermarket—all one word

supersede—means to "set" over, not "yield" over, so it's supersede

take—see "bring"

transatlantic—also, now, transpacific, and transpolar

ukulele—not ukelele or ukalele

underprivileged—no "le*d*ge" to stand on

under way—there is no such word as "underway"

unique—avoid overuse; also note there are no degrees of uniqueness

up to date—"We must bring our records up to date."
up-to-date—the *adjective* form: "This is our most up-to-date directory." "She's an old-fashioned girl with an up-to-date vocabulary."

venetian blinds—lower case V

veracious—truthful
voracious—insatiable, ravenous, greedy in eating

veracity—truthfulness
verity—truth

vertical—not "verticle"
vehicle—not "vehical"

vital—use this word sparingly

vice president—hyphen no longer needed

weird, wield, yield—note positions of *i* and *e*

whiskey—often spelled this way when referring to American types; Scotch drops the *e*; so does Canadian; plural in all cases is "whiskies"

Xmas—never write it that way for publication anywhere

VII.

Typographic Style

Punctuation

A standard style for dashes in *typewritten* copy is a pair of hyphens with a space on either end, like this:

He stressed the importance of reaching the best solution - - on social and economic grounds - - of the problem of a post-war . . .

Here is "the inside-outside story" of where to put punctuation marks in relation to closing quotation marks:

Figuring out where to put periods, commas, parentheses and other punctuation when a closing quote wants to occupy the same space is not easy, but it follows completely logical thinking in all respects save one, namely:

Periods and commas always go inside the quote marks.

This flat rule, which has bothered many well-trained secretaries and teachers of English, is based upon typographical considerations (appearance). Editors long ago decided they had to agree with printers that there is some esthetic clumsiness and unattractiveness about terminating a sentence "this way". Both the quote and the period seem rather disembodied. It would be the same with a comma.

There is one exception: where single and double quotes occur together and in conjunction with a period or comma, as:

There are such earthy references as Hans von Bulow's remark about "the beery complacency with which Herr Richter conducts 'Die Meistersinger'."

The other punctuation marks, possibly because they are typographically "taller," are placed (in relation to quotes) on the basis of grammatical logic. *Parentheses*, for example, go *outside* the final period when an entire sentence is parenthetical; but *inside* when only the final portion of the sentence is parenthetical.

EXAMPLES:

(It was later explained that no priority order had been issued.)

. . . they will be running every day (though not on Sundays).

Interrogation points, exclamation points, semicolons and colons are treated in the same way. That is, their position with respect to the quotes is determined by whether they apply to the *whole thought* or just to the *quoted word* or section.

EXAMPLES:

He kept asking, "Where's my catcher's glove?"

How many couturiers honestly approve of the "mod look"?

She replied, "I've never been so insulted in my life!"

Actually, it turned out there were nearly 100 students who admitted they had taken psychedelic "trips"!

The senator said, "I still feel there was nothing immoral about having those testimonial dinners"; even so, he indicated there would be none during his next campaign.

The astronaut denied he had ever felt that he was just a "fifth wheel"; he insisted there had been no hurt feelings.

This is the procedure when you find yourself on the "hot seat": keep cool, demand to have a lawyer present, look your inquisitor square in the eye . . .

VICE PRESIDENTIAL TROUBLE. In recent years it has become

fashionable (though punctuationally hybrid) to refer to certain
company officers as vice president–sales, vice president–production, vice president–public relations and so on. Try to avoid
these half-baked hyphenations whenever possible by putting the
adjective in front of the v. p., making it read, for example, sales
vice president and financial vice president. However, sometimes
a client insists on the hyphenated style; when this happens, one
compromise is to make it a dash instead of a hyphen, but *omit*
the spaces that normally would be at either end of the dash, like
this: "Last April he was named vice president–sales and since
August has been in charge of . . ."

Note that this "long hyphen" usage is different from the standard style for typewriter dashes, described in the first paragraph
in this section on punctuation.

This same technique, of a dash without spacing, is useful also
when two multiword names are to be hyphenated.

EXAMPLES:

. . . to be called the Edward M. Kahn–Emko Ribbon Company.
. . . will be built by Nuclear Products–Erco Division of ACF
    Industries.

Two hyphenated-words combinations that themselves *should*
be linked can be effectively handled this way: "The shells are
produced by the hot-cup/cold-draw method." That diagonal line
is usually called a slash. Its more formal name is "virgule."

DOT'S NICE! When you use a series of three periods as a punctuation device, BE SURE that you use them with SPACES
BETWEEN the dots. It's a good idea to be sparing and discriminating in the use of this device, for it is easy to misuse
and overuse. It should be reserved for occasions where you
mean to indicate a very marked pause or break.

Note that when you use the spaced dots punctuation *between*
sentences you need four dots, all told, the first being the period
that terminates the first sentence.

Because this spaced-dot technique has become so popular in

various column-style writings, the string of dots has lost some of the recognition it once had as an indicator of ellipsis — to show that, in a particular passage of quotation from another document, some wordage was being omitted. Therefore, some writers prefer to use three spaced asterisks in cases of ellipsis.

UNSPACED DOTS are something quite different. In typed copy they are equivalent to what printers call leaders, which have a specific typographic function and are used in tabulated matter, box scores, etc., as in the following example of tabulation of Suggestion System payoffs:

	No. Sug.	Total Awards
Ed Ek	5	$4,300
Amos Mergenthaler	3	3,000
Bill May	3	2,700
John Gutenberg	2	2,200
R. Hoe	2	1,850

FLOW—In the interest of better "flow" we omit the second of two so-called complementary commas except where the comma is needed for other reasons.

EXAMPLE:

Robert Smith was named superintendent of the Schenley Industries, Inc. plant at Lawrenceburg, Ind. on May 17, 1958 and has built an extraordinary safety record there.

NOTE that "Inc." "Ind." and "1958" all MIGHT be followed by commas under a liberal comma policy. When faced with such a construction, ask yourself if there would be a comma if the "Inc." or the "Ind." or the "1958" were not there. Obviously the sentence above would read simply: Robert Smith was named superintendent of the Schenley Industries plant at Lawrenceburg on May 17 and has built an extraordinary safety record there.

CONVERSE EXAMPLE:

Robert Smith, president of Schenley Industries, Inc., which has a plant in Lawrenceburg, Ind., took office on May 17, 1958, a day that will be long remembered.

We do not use a comma between a man's name and "Jr."

MOST NEGLECTED of all punctuational units probably is the *semicolon*. Often it can do a far better job than either "and" or "but" in indicating relationship between two halves of a sentence.

Discussing a big torpedo contract, a company official said:

This is extremely attractive business for our company, and a high-volume product of this nature provides our ordnance division with long-term stability.

The "and" connector here is not accurate, because the long-term stability attained through this high-volume product *is* what makes this business "extremely attractive." Thus it might be defensible to use the word "because" as a connector; if you do not wish to be quite that specific in pointing to cause and effect, just use a semicolon instead of the comma, and scrub the "and."

Capitalization

Be sparing in use of capitals in titles of company or association officers. It is true that newspapers have become more liberal about initial caps in recent years, but it is easy to make a release look overly commercial by loading it with capitals in references to Sales Managers, Superintendents, and so forth.

Capitalize:

* Full names of societies, clubs, associations, colleges, etc.:
    First Presbyterian Church
    Northern Electric's Twenty-Year Club
    Princeton University
    Senate Military Affairs Committee (but not subcommittee)
    United States military decorations: Congressional Medal of
        Honor, Bronze Star, Purple Heart, etc.
* Names of streets, avenues, boulevards, stations, airports, etc.:
    Wentworth Avenue
    22nd Street
    Grand Concourse
    Warwick Hotel
    125th Street Station
    Palace Theater
    La Guardia Airport
* "Company" and "Corporation" when in conjunction with the full name. In all names of business organizations, use the style used by the company itself with respect to capitalizing, use of ampersand, use of "Inc." or "Incorporated," and so forth. N.B., however: do *not* follow company typographic style (in releases) to the extent of capitalizing *all* the letters in a name when the letters form a word. "X-Y-Z Corp." is allowable but *not* "MY-TEE FINE Co."
* Names of political parties—Republican, Democrat, Democratic, Liberal, etc.—but not the word "party."
* Political and company titles when *preceding* the name: President John W. Smith (but John W. Smith, president of, etc.). Exception: in reference to the President of the United States, "President" is capitalized regardless of whether it is before or after the name, or even if the name is not used in the same sentence, as: "The President returned to the White House tanned and rested."

• The Bible, when referring to the Holy Bible. But lower-case it when the word is used in a figurative sense.

• West Germany, East Germany—but western Europe, eastern Europe, except where reference implies political unity; South Texas, East Texas, West Texas and some parts of other states where a definite regional flavor is involved in the subject matter (e.g., Southern and Northern California, Southern Illinois). Also Upper Peninsula (of Michigan) . . . but make it upstate New York, western Massachusetts.

• Titles of books, plays, movies, ships. Also, put them in quotation marks in first reference; in subsequent references capitalizing suffices.

• College degrees when using the initials only, as A.B. and LL.D. But lower-case them when they are spelled out: "He received a bachelor of arts degree from Princeton." (Incidentally, do not write "Mr. Jones received *his* master's degree," etc., unless the story has already made it clear he has one. Just say "received *a* master's degree.")

• North, South, East and West and combinations thereof when referring to sections of the country—but not when used simply as directions, as:

He headed north at a rapid pace.

She was a true daughter of the South.

The southern route lay near the equator.

Fraternities are less prominent in Eastern colleges.

• Names of all nationalities and all races: British, Indian, Negro, Caucasian.

Variables

GEOGRAPHICAL NAMES—oceans, rivers, mountains, etc.—use lower case for the generic word except where it precedes the proper noun (Lake Louise, Sea of Azov) and except where there is a distinctive identity as a "place" beyond mere geographic identification (Devil's Island, Ellis Island) or where the proper name preceding could be regarded as merely descriptive (Thousand Islands, Broad Lake, Rocky Mountains).

ANIMALS. Follow a good desk dictionary on capitalization of breeds and types of animals: Hereford cattle—but white-face cattle; Airedale—but collie; Clydesdale, Percheron, Shetland—but shire, mustang, pinto; Angora—but mohair.

FAMILY MEMBERS should be capitalized when used abstractly or symbolically or in direct address: "Pies like *Mother* used to make." "Ask *Dad*, he knows." "Barbara said, 'May I go out to swim, *Mother*?'" BUT: "A boy's best friend is his *mother*." . . . "Next time *Daughter* wants to borrow the family car." BUT: "We often let our *daughter* borrow the car."
"Sir" should be capitalized in direct address, as: "I'll take the high road, Sir." But not necessarily in "yes sir."

WINES. Refer to a good desk dictionary for capitalization of wine names. They are difficult to guess correctly; generally capitalization is related to the name's springing from a place-name, but not necessarily. Burgundy, Chianti, Rhine, Chablis, Graves, for examples, are capped on this basis, but not zinfandel, sauterne, champagne, port (from Oporto), sherry (from Jerez). Merely descriptive, of course, are vin rosé and claret.

Do Not Capitalize:

. . . board of directors (except in letters or annual report, etc.)
winter, summer, spring, fall
a.m. or p.m.
"ex" and "former," even when combined with a capitalized title, as: ex-King Alfonso, former Ambassador Gerard
federal (except as part of a proper name) . . . government

Note: Although a capital *C* is used in either Company or Corporation when first giving a concern's full name, those words should not be capitalized when standing alone in subsequent mentions. For example:

James B. Altimeter, president of the Indianapolis-Burnside *Company*, today announced formation of a subsidiary. . . . He explained that the *company* had been considering such a move. . . . It was recalled that the Burnside *company* long had been affiliated. . . .

The question of CAPITALIZING the words "Earth" and "Moon" has been causing much pencil chewing on copy desks in these 1960s since Man has been seriously contemplating going from one of those bodies to the other and ultimately did.

It is probably not wise to try to make an absolutely rigid rule about it, because the nature of references to each varies so widely. The recommended course is to stick to the "down style," i.e., "earth" and "moon," except when the nature of the story seems to justify the initial caps. Times change and, as Grandpa often observed, "the earth do move!"

Call Him Mister?

In newspaper circles generally the use of the prefix "Mr." is considered unnecessarily formal. Of course it is *never* used in the first reference to a man, i.e., when you're giving his first name or initials.

In second and subsequent references—so goes the dominant newspaper policy—"Mr." is used only

1. In connection with *and Mrs.*
2. In obituaries or other references to someone who has died
3. In reference to a clergyman or the President
4. In quoted matter

There are exceptions. Some papers use "Mr." for everyone

except sports performers and persons whose conduct is unmistakably ungentlemanly or persons in difficulty with the law. But such papers are a small minority.

Liberal use of "Mr." in a public relations release could cause editors to get the impression that a subject (person) is being wreathed in more dignity than is quite necessary.

Conclusion: The policy indicated in the paragraph with the numbers is recommended.

Company Divisions and Schools Within Universities

Two areas in which it is difficult to lay down rigid rules on capitalization are the names of *divisions* of industrial corporations, and the names of *schools* of particular academic pursuits that are parts of universities.

The problem arises because, in each area, although the names of most such divisions and schools are quite routinely descriptive — carburetor division, maintenance department, research group, school of medicine, engineering school — not all of them are that generic. Some embody undeniably proper nouns — the University of Pennsylvania's Wharton School of Finance, Chemetron Corporation's NCG division.

The recommended policy is to stay with the "down style" except where there are strong reasons for going to the capital letters — and any temptation to capitalize the word "division" itself should be especially resisted.

Abbreviation

Abbreviate:

• Names of states when they follow names of cities, as: "Mary Foster of Binghamton, N.Y. was a guest."

• Names of states, always, in datelines. (Exceptions to both the above: Alaska, Hawaii, Idaho, Iowa, Ohio, Maine and Utah are not abbreviated.)

• The months of January, February, August, September, October, November and December—not only in datelines, but in text when showing an *actual date,* as: "Pearl Harbor was attacked Dec. 7, 1941." "He returned to the Toledo plant last Jan. 10."

• Easily recognized standard names such as YMCA, WCTU, AFL-CIO, VFW, GOP, NASA.

• Military titles, at the person's first mention in a story, and when first name or initials are used, as: "More than 3,000 persons heard Brig. Gen. Raymond F. Fowler speak at the Armory." But in subsequent mentions spell it out, as: "After the parade, General Fowler called upon the Pure Oats Company's foremen's association."

• Political titles "Representative" and "Senator," in the same pattern as above, viz.: "Rep. Edwin L. Higgins (R-N.Y.) was absent." But: "Upon his return to the floor, Representative Higgins voted." (But do not use such constructions as: Bourke Hickenlooper, sen. from Iowa.)

• "Professor" to "Prof." in first reference, "Professor" thereafter (same pattern as for Gen., Rep., Sen.).

First reference should be spelled out in such locations as "miles per hour," "gallons per minute," "inches per second" (tape speed) and "pounds per square inch" except in matter aimed at technical publications. Subsequent references may be mph, gpm, ips, psi, etc.

Do Not Abbreviate:

Avenue, street, boulevard.

Christian names, as Wm. for William; Geo. for George, etc.— except where subject himself prefers that.

Christmas to the Xmas form.

Per cent, except where used in tabulations.

Cents, except in strictly financial releases.

Names of states when they appear in context. For example: "Four citizens of West Virginia visited Steubenville last night."

Names of months when used in context and without specific date, as: "This was the coldest February on record." (And never abbreviate March, April, May, June, July, even in a dateline.)

President, secretary, treasurer, chairman, etc.

Figures

Use spelled-out words for numbers below 10; use figures for 10 and up.

EXCEPTIONS:

When more than one number, some above and some below 10, appear in one sentence, use either figures or spelled-out numbers, whichever is most appropriate in the context, but be consistent within each sentence. For example:

There were 5 to 20 torpedoes on each landing barge.

On the reviewing stand were seven senators and fourteen representatives.

On birthdays, use the spelled-out form regardless of whether it's a little boy or a Toscanini. "Toscanini marked his eighty-second birthday by rehearsing Brahms." But in stating ages of persons, use figures: "Betty Blake, 3, got a surprise when she went wading." "Mr. Jones was elected president when he was 39."

Use Figures For:

Hours of the day, as: 7:30 p.m.

Dimensions, degrees of temperature, per cent, dates, votes, times and distances in athletic events, dollars and cents when used with symbols, etc., as:

a life raft 4 by 9 feet. (Do not use the 4 x 9 form.)

a cabinet reaching 6 below zero.

a 3 per cent increase.

Manganese sold at $1.25 per 8-pound unit.

Do not bother with "nd," "th" and the like in dates when the month is given. Make it simply July 5.

Use figures when writing time in terms of a.m. or p.m. or with "o'clock." As: "Dedication will be at 7:30 p.m." "It was 4 o'clock before the captain got an answer to his radiogram." And, of course, do not use "o'clock" in the same phrase with a.m. or p.m.; nor should you use a.m. or p.m. when you mention "morning" or "evening."

Do not start a sentence with a figure. Either start it with some other expression or spell out in full the number. (Note: In copyreading and proofreading, a circle around a figure means to spell it out; conversely, a circle around a spelled-out number means to convert it to figures.)

Save time, space and potential confusion by omitting *unneeded* zeroes in time and money references, as:

Chapel begins at 8 a.m. [not 8:00 a.m.].

The new catalog sells for $1, the manual for $1.75.

Hyphens

Use hyphens sparingly—there will be plenty of them in carefully punctuated copy even if you try to be conservative in their use—but do use them where they're called for.

The modern trend is toward running together many word combinations that have traditionally been regarded as hyphenations. Viz:

> transatlantic
> cooperation
> semifinal
> antediluvian

However, the hyphen is useful in making clear that combinations of two or more words are being used adjectively, as a unit, in modifying another. Note the difference between

Mayor Jones said he wanted a better housing campaign this year

and

Mayor Jones said he wanted a better-housing campaign this year.

Or

He was astonished to see a man eating tiger in the mess hall

when what is meant is

He was astonished to see a man-eating tiger in the mess hall.

Do not use the hyphen to indicate a linkage when the two words are quite commonly used in that manner. For example:

> long distance (phone call)
> high tension (wire)
> vice president

Strictly speaking, such two-word adjectives as these *should* be hooked together with a hyphen, but these and many others are so familiar in such couplings that hyphenation is unnecessary.

It is also unnecessary to use the hyphen in two-word combinations where the first word has the adverbial "ly" ending, because the construction in itself indicates that the two words are to be taken together. For example:

It was a highly controversial subject.

Thinly dressed aborigines stared at the troops.

Despite the injunction to use the hyphen sparingly, DO NOT be afraid to use two hyphens when a three-word phrase is acting as a single modifier. It does not make sense, for example, to refer to a 30-year old man or to a 30 year-old one; he is a man who is 30 years old, so the sensible way to write it is 30-year-old man.

Similarly, there is no validity to the expression multi-million dollar program; make it either multi-million-dollar or (preferably) multimillion-dollar.

Examples of the difference a hyphen or two can make:

It was pointed out that these new packaging techniques eliminate the day-old cake problem.

Well, if the *cake problem* had been bothering them for only one day it couldn't have been so terribly important, could it? (It's the problem of day-old cake, so "day" and "old" and "cake" *all* have to be hooked together by hyphens when you use them as an adjectival unit as in the quoted sentence.)

C. S. Stephens, non-food can expert for the company, said—

This makes Stephens a can expert who somehow gets along without food. What he really is is an expert on non-food cans. If you insist on the super-compact adjectival form you have to make it "non-food-can expert." This is logical, but clumsy, and it has, indeed, a vaguely uncomplimentary sound. So why not call him the company's expert on non-food cans? [Incidentally, as a progress footnote: It is possible to find "nonfood" in one or two of the most recent dictionaries.]

Following luncheon there will be a series of small, round table discussions.

These would be conferences held around—or about—small, comma round tables, eh? (Drop the comma and hyphenate "round-table.")

The control system is used to regulate a multiple head drilling
    machine that . . .

Any time you want any heads drilled be sure and use this
control system! A hyphen would make it clear, even at first
glance, that this is a drilling machine *equipped with more than
one head,* not a machine used for head drilling.

There has been a strong trend in recent years toward making
single words out of many that formerly were compounds involving suffixes, like *mid, non, trans, inter, over, under.*

It's still, as always, a good idea to consult the dictionary when
you are in doubt, but generally you can "lean" toward closing
up such terms, when they are generally familiar ones.

A few examples:

midsummer, midwinter, midweek, Midwest, midair, midday,
    midterm, midrange, midstream, midtown.

But it's possible to overdo it. For instance, when the second
part of the compound is a proper name—as *mid-January, trans-
Siberian*—leave that hyphen in. Notable exceptions—or quasi-
exceptions*—to this are, of course, transatlantic and transpacific,
now accepted although many feel it was the height of irrever-
ent expediency to devalue the identity of the two biggest things
in the world this way.

Almost any recent dictionary will all but astound most con-
sulters by the large array of words that start with "non" and
proceed without benefit of hyphen. Here are a few, not necessarily as an endorsement or because you are likely to need
them very often, but just to give an idea of how strong the trend
has become:

nonabsolute   noncanniballistic (!) nonmigratory nontheatrical
nonadherent noncondensation   nonkosher   nonretroactive
nonathletic   nonfossiliferous   nonvertical   nontyrannical

---

* Quasi, on the other hand, is never "run in" with the word it modifies.
Other Latin-derived combining forms, notably *ultra* and *supra,* have been
so well absorbed that it is quite rare that anyone feels the need to separate
them from the rest of the words in which they are combined. *Infra* is getting
this kind of acceptance, too, though it appears in relative few combinations,
notably the easily misread (and easily mispronounced) *infrared.* (One p.r.
house has a rule that, in radio and TV scripts, this one has to be hyphenated.)

Apostrophes

Do not use the apostrophe in such well-established abbreviations as: phone, Frisco, varsity. (But use it in 'chute, not yet familiar enough as a shortening of parachute.)

In cases like Westchester Teachers' Association, Farmers Bank of Newcastle, Amalgamated Bricklayers' Union of Albany and Elks Club (specific organizations), be guided by the practice of the organization or company itself in use of the apostrophe. (Also, Mother's Day; Dad's Day.)

In expressions dealing with the duration or length of a trip, or a delay, the problem of "to apostrophize or not to apostrophize, and where to put it," almost always can be solved easily by not bothering with *either* plurals or apostrophes. Just say "a five-mile hike," "a 10-minute walk," "a three-hour delay."

The apostrophe is necessary in such names and phrases as "men's department," "women's wear" and "children's hour"— because there are no such words as "mens," "womens," "childrens." And, by the same token, no such words as "mens'," "womens'," "childrens' "!

No apostrophe is necessary in the possessive form of pronouns: ours, yours, hers, theirs, its, whose. ("It's" and "who's" are *contractions,* not *possessives.*)

Do not use the *second* apostrophe in such expressions as "the gay '90's." Just make it "the gay '90s."

Use the apostrophe in giving college or school class years, as: "class of '98" and "Edgar Allan Poe, Princeton '14."

Form the possessive of words ending in *s,* or in an *s sound,* by adding the apostrophe only, as:

It was Jones' turn at bat. The chairman said Bendix' attitude was sound.

Per Cent and Percentages

"Per cent" is used as two words (though some recent dictionaries make it "percent").

Use it spelled out, always, in preference to the % sign (except in tabulations and headlines.)

BE SURE you are on firm ground, mathematically, when translating figures on increase or decrease (of production, sales, etc.) into percentages.

N.B.: If you do four times as much business this year as last, you have not shown a 400 per cent increase, but a 300 per cent one.

N.B. Do not use loosely and inaccurately the prepositions "of" and "over" (or "more than") in telling of increases; BECAUSE the statement "our business this year was 150 per cent *over* [or *more than*] last year's" means we did *two*-and-a-half times as much, WHEREAS the statement "our business this year was 150 per cent *of* last year's means we did *one*-and-a-half times as much.

REMEMBER: It is mathematically and physically impossible for anything to decrease by more than 100 per cent!

REMEMBER: Because of the confusability of this subject, it is almost always more effective, in making clear that a sizable increase or gain has been scored, to say it in terms of "times as much" instead of expressing it percentagewise. For example, "nearly three times as many people visited Expo 67" is more effective than "187 per cent more persons visited Expo 67" although each statement could be based upon the same statistics.

VIII.

Making
It
Look
Right

In the public relations business, unless you're one of those rare and prophetic "medicine men" who can command substantial fees for tossing off two or three earth-shaking ideas a year, you have to have "a product."

Indeed, even the most brilliant ideas have to be put into transmittable words—audible or readable, or both.

Your "product" is, of course, what you write. And in this day and age when everything comes in such elegant, neat, convenient and persuasive packaging, the public relations product had better be well packaged. It had better look good, to begin with.

Even the most correct, clever and potentially persuasive prose will not succeed if it doesn't get heard or read. You must make sure your copy is presented in a way that reassures the recipient that here is something worthy of his consideration.

Here, then, are some basic guides to the physical appearance of release copy:

Physical Appearance
of Release Copy

STANDARD form for upper-left corner:

From: Carl Byoir & Associates, Inc.
      800 Second Avenue, 986-6100
      New York, N.Y. 10017

For: THE BENDIX CORPORATION

DATELINE—RELEASE LINE PROCEDURE
(Release lines in upper right corner)

A. On a story about a specific event that takes place at a specific time, such as a speech, meeting, press demonstration, unveiling . . .

> For release after (specify the hour)
> Wednesday, Oct. 12, 1969

The dateline on such a story would of course bear the date Oct. 12.

B. On a story where no precise "hour" release time is appropriate—such as a new product announcement without demonstration—but you definitely want to be available first to *morning* newspapers . . .

> For release
> in morning papers of
> Wednesday, Oct. 12, 1969

AND you put Oct. *11* in the dateline.

C. Same type of story as B, but you wish to make it available first to *afternoon papers* . . .

> For release
> in afternoon papers of
> Wednesday, Oct. 12, 1969

AND you put Oct. *12* in the dateline.

NOTE WELL that the three forms are shown above as used on releases *that bear datelines*. Always, of course, the *time reference* in the lead *must agree* with the date that is in the *dateline*.

SPECIAL NOTE: Regulations of the Securities and Exchange Commission require that any news releases on behalf of publicly held companies, dealing with earnings reports, dividend actions and stock splits, or indeed any developments, such as an acquisition, change in top executive personnel, significant expansion, or other matter that conceivably would *have an effect on investment decisions*, must be made available to the press as soon as the action that is the subject of the news release is taken. Do not mark any such story for release at any future designated day or hour; it must be, literally, FOR IMMEDIATE RELEASE.

On releases that DO NOT BEAR A DATELINE, the same forms of upper-right "release line" should be used. Note, however, (especially when you are removing a dateline in making a revised version of a story) that the *time reference* in the lead must be *in agreement* with the date that the publication bears.

To illustrate: If you had a story with a WATERBURY DATELINE, about an event that took place Tuesday, Feb. 11 and was for release to the New York morning papers of Wednesday, Feb. 12, the time reference to the event would be "today." . . . BUT . . . if for some reason you decided to hand the same story *without* the dateline to the same newspapers for Wednesday's editions, you would have to change the time reference in the story to "yesterday."

Caution—Caution—Morning -Paper Time References

A hard fact of newspaper life that far too many people have difficulty remembering is:

Every dateline in any morning newspaper ALWAYS bears the date of the PRECEDING day (except in extraordinary cases where something like an earthquake occurs and justifies the paper's getting into the paper a dispatch that actually was filed subsequent to the preceding midnight; in those cases the paper does use the same date in the dateline as its day of publication, but puts in parentheses the name of the day, as confirmation).

By the same token, no morning newspaper will ever have a first-paragraph time reference, in a *nondatelined* story, to something's having been "announced today," or "said today," or anything's having been done—past tense—"today." The reason: such a *past-tense-today* reference would be saying that this statement was made sometime between the preceding midnight and the time that morning paper landed on your doorstep, at 6 A.M. or earlier—an obvious absurdity.

Further Notes on Datelines and Release Lines

TRADE PAPER versions of spot news stories should, of course, be restenciled to ease the time restrictions. In those cases where it is appropriate one can use a dateline (AKRON, OHIO, for instance) *without* any date. Judgment will dictate how the time element is handled in the first paragraph; in most cases it is preferable to leave out the reference to "announced today" and just say that such-and-such a device *"has been* introduced" or words to that effect. (Be sure such versions carry the full date *somewhere on them.*)

EVERGREEN feature stories, which are usable any time, should have this same *undated* dateline, if a dateline is necessary at all—and of course no "todays" in the lead paragraph (except in a figure-of-speech context like "today's typical hardware store bears little resemblance to . . ."). Examples of state mention in datelines:

For spot news release:

CHICAGO, March 30—A plea that the effect of scientific progress . . .
or
ALTOONA, Pa., March 30—Resumption of board-track racing was . . .

For evergreen feature where no release date is specified:

PHILADELPHIA—The history of aviation has been marked by . . .
or
SIOUX FALLS, S.D.—The President's annual visit to the Black Hills . . .

NOTE: It is strongly recommended that on features of this kind, at least the month and year be printed flush left at the end of the story.

DO NOT use the name of the state in the case of really big cities; also leave out the name of the state in case of even small cities when the release is going only to papers within that state. For example, a general release from a nonmetropolitan community:

LAWRENCEBURG, Ind., April 22—Four hundred new penicillin cultures were developed here within . . .

BUT the same story, if for circulation in Indiana only:

LAWRENCEBURG, April 22—Four hundred new penicillin cultures . . .

WHAT'S A 'REALLY BIG' CITY? The two big wire services do not undertake to prescribe those cities deemed so recognizable that it is unnecessary to mention the state. They let the wire editors play it by ear. Generally, all the "big league" cities, and a few others, are used without state mention. There are, of course, Cleveland, Tenn.; Pittsburg (no h), Kan.; Rome, N.Y.; Naples, Fla., and any number of Washingtons, but it is assumed that the state *will* be mentioned with any of those, and if the state is *not* mentioned it's the "the" city that's meant.

DO NOT send out releases for publication with the "Nov. 00—" style.

THE MONTHS of March, April, May, June and July should be spelled out in datelines; all others abbreviated.

IN DATELINES, all state names are abbreviated except Alaska, Hawaii, Idaho, Iowa, Ohio, Maine and Utah.
N.B.: Somewhere on every piece of copy there must be a date, complete as to month and year even if you don't want to indicate the day. This is important, because subject matter has a way of recurring, and it almost always proves highly desirable to know exactly when a previous version of a story or background memo was prepared. (It's amazing, when a piece of copy is filed by subject matter, how soon even the author of it forgets what year it was produced!)

Headline Styles

One of the typical and annoying excesses of publicity copy is its tendency toward headlines that are unrealistically long. A study of metropolitan papers shows no instances where there is a unit count higher than 16 in any of the top three lines in a two-deck "top" head—mostly the counts are around 13 to 15.

Even in the smaller, two-line heads (single deck) the counts run more to the 16–19 units range than the 22–25 that is often seen on releases.

On longer stories of feature type, heads suitable for setting in two-column measure are indicated. The average count on these in metropolitan papers is in the 25–28 range.

Here are typical headline formats:

For a standard, straight-news type of release:

PRE-SPUN TIRES
ON WHEELS GIVE
EXTRA LANDINGS
Cleveland Engineer Gives Report
on Self-starting Device
to S.A.E. Meeting

NEVER exceed 16 units in main deck; nor 35 units in top line of second.

It is often advisable to omit the second deck, especially where its use would necessitate going to a second page. For stories of feature type, running 200 words or more, a two-line head suitable for two-columns use in the paper is appropriate, like this:

PROBLEM WINDOW? NO SIR, NEVER!
NOT IF YOUR DECORATOR'S CLEVER

For short items—8 to 15 typed lines—of either spot news or feature character, a two-line head suitable for 1-column newspaper use, such as:

BUSY STORK GIVES
BUSINESS THE BIRD

The following is a headline style that is fairly popular with papers, is easy to write from the "count" standpoint and lends itself equally well to sober or gay items:

QUEENS FOR A DAY

Early Greeks Were First to Pay
Homage to Mother

And here is a "double-jointed" headline style that is easy to write, lends itself to light language and is suitable for a fairly long, feature-type piece:

Cat's Pajamas!
**EVERYTHING FROM ALPACA TO ZYLON
ON VIEW AT FELINE FASHION SHOW**

New Deal In Wheels:
**TRAVEL ON MOON WILL REQUIRE
SOMETHING NEW UNDER THE SUN**

BE CAREFUL, and MAKE SURE, that you do not put something in the headline that is not in the story.

TRY TO AVOID using any word more than once in a headline (but don't indulge in far-fetched synonyms in doing so).

ALWAYS use single quote marks in headlines (also in top lines of photo captions).

DO NOT "split" two words that are, in context, tightly complementary, by having them fall on separate lines in the headline. For example:

**LECTURE ON ATOM
SAVING METHOD IS
GIVEN AT SCHOOL**

DO NOT start a headline with a verb. For example:

**DISCOVER METHOD
FOR GETTING OIL
FROM UTAH SHALE**

Some newspapers have tended to relax on this rule in recent years, but there still are many editors who regard this as slipshod, ineffective headline writing, and you should not risk incurring their scorn by offering such copy. There is a special reason for avoiding this construction when the verb is a plural one, in that the headline *may* appear to be *exhorting* the reader to some course of action. For example:

**READ TRANSCRIPT
OF MABEL JONES'
DIARY IN COURT**

Here is an almost unbelievable example of disregarding this rule, an actual headline in a New York paper about a shot-in-the-back assassination in Mississippi:

SLAY NAACP LEADER!

Photo Captions

A two-part type of caption sheet is recommended. A small, "tab" part—containing the standard "From" wording, the negative number of the photo and a "slug line"—is permanently pasted on the back of the photo; a larger part, containing caption and cutlines and negative number, folds over the face of the photo.

The negative number should appear on both parts.

(This system makes it easy for the editor to tear off the actual caption and yet leave adequate identification permanently on the back of the photo—and the negative numbers on each half make it easy to match up or trace.)

Preferred Caption Format

FROZEN ASSETS of the refreshment business were quickly melted when this ice-cream wagon tipped over on Sunrise Boulevard at high noon today. Neighborhood kids speedily liquidated all the stock not taken care of by the sun's rays.

The ideal sought in the above format is to have a couple of all-cap words that in themselves constitute a catchy clue to the subject of the photo and yet also constitute the opening words of a sentence that gets quickly to the point. When this is impossible, it is allowable to use this alternative form:

FROZEN ASSETS—Butchers at the Elmdale A & P are shown as they wielded pick-axes instead of cleavers to pry loose provisions that were frozen solid in cases when refrigerating mechanism went on rampage.

Allowable Caption Format

SWEETS TO THE SWEET
Monica Dextrose (left) of the films is shown breaking a bottle of corn syrup over a new sugar cane grinding machine in dedication ceremonies at Wingdale Tech, etc.

PERSONNEL type of caption (for strictly head shots, as in connection with appointment to new office, etc.):

ROGER JONES (above) has been elected sales vice president of the External Combustion Co.

DO NOT use the "label" or *nonsentence* type of construction in captions for such situations as above. That is, do NOT say "Roger Jones (above), *who* has been . . ."

A sensible style in identifying persons in photos by position is to put such terms as left, left to right and so forth *in parentheses* and spelled out. Make sure that you put such parenthetic reference right *next* to the person's *name*.

Photo in Series, Picture Stories

Frequently it will be desirable to send a series—or an assortment —of photos on a given subject.

In the case of a *series*, where the pictures ideally would appear in definite *sequence*, a format like this is recommended:

> MOUNTAIN-TOP MAGIC (Four-picture series—No. 1)
> A half-dozen scientists live an almost monastic existence the year-round on the crest of blustery Mount Washington in New Hampshire, devoting themselves to studies to make flying safer. [Brief "over-all introduction" type of caption . . . followed by:]
>
> (I) THIS PHOTO SHOWS: Parka-clad observer on precarious perch reading anemometer while De-Icers pulsate . . .

In the case of a set of pictures having no particular sequence, a similar format can well be employed, but with these differences:

> MOUNTAIN-TOP MAGIC (One of four pictures)
> A half-dozen scientists . . . [same as in other form].
> PERCHED PRECARIOUSLY as he takes reading of anemometer . . .

REMEMBER: That although frequently photos are sent out in connection with a fairly important news release that tells a story more completely than can be done with cutlines, the captions on such photos always should be factually self-sufficient as to the "who, when, where, etc.," because they are sure to get separated from the story sooner or later.

A TIP ON CAPTION WRITING: *Look* at the picture while you write the caption, and write it from the standpoint of giving the reader the quickest, clearest explanation you can of what the picture is about. Resist any temptation to start by spelling out the background situation and then gradually working up to saying something about what the reader is looking at. Make captions quick and helpful and bright, and *weave in* the company or other identification, instead of writing that plug and then just sticking on the other information.

DON'TS for Caption Writing

DON'T use the phrase "looking on" if you can possibly avoid it—and you certainly can avoid it if you try. (It's bad enough to *have* some person in a photo who is not doing anything more important than "looking on," but let us not emphasize his superfluousness by that give-away phrase.)

DON'T use such phrases as "while Soandso beams approval" or "looks on admiringly." It's old-fashioned and trite—and the picture itself will testify to the person's beamishness.

DON'T insert the gratuitous "pretty" in a caption before the pretty girl's name. It sounds as though you don't trust the picture to convey the correct impression. She's undoubtedly pretty or we wouldn't be using her, and if our picture failed to capture her beauty we'd throw it away and use one that did!

BE SURE every caption bears a date.

Articles in Captions

There seems to be an impression that newspaper style requires *nonuse of articles* ("the," "a," "an," etc.) in picture captions.

This is not true. Brevity is fine, but leaving out the's, a's and an's is not the way to achieve brevity. You achieve brevity by skill, and by thoughtful and determined writing (including, of course, *re*writing).

It is true that you can make many captions shorter by using telegraphese. But in many cases ruthless elimination of articles makes sentences clumsy and unclear.

Write the best caption you possibly can, and whittle it down as tightly as you possibly can, but don't write completely article-less captions.

Tips for Typers

Standardize margin widths at 10 units from left; 12 to 8 units from right.

Indent paragraph beginnings 8 units.

These margins apply to all newspaper and magazine copy, regardless of length of story. The reason for this is that actual newsroom copy is always written "full width" of the copy paper, no matter how tiny the item—and you don't want your copy to look much different from the staff-written copy the newspaper folk are dealing with day by day.

Familiarize yourself with at least the rudimentary copyreading and proofreading marks, such as:

Three lines under a letter, like this: the . . . means to capitalize it.

A diagonal line through a letter, like this: B . . . means to lower-case it.

A circle around a written-out number, like this: "he captured (seventeen) Vietcong," means that seventeen should be converted to 17.

A circle around a figure, like this: "he captured (7) Vietcong," means that 7 should be written out, seven.

(Those two examples, as corrected, represent the general rule as to putting numbers in words or figures; i.e., use *words* for numbers *below* 10, use figures for 10 *and above*.)*

* There are, of course, exceptions to the figures-words rule. See "Figures" pages 144-145.

Also, a circle around a word, or an abbreviation, means to transcribe it "the other way." That is, a circle around "Co." would mean to change it to "company"; conversely, a circle around "company" would mean to make it "Co."

The symbol for deletion—of a word, a letter, etc.—is a sort of lop-eared script *e* like this: ℯ

"The CYO is stepping up its program for under/privileged children." (Delete the hyphen.)

"Tr" written in the margin, coupled with a waved line ("Joe Logan lived in a concrete house") means to *transpose*, either letters or words, or even whole lines. It usually is obvious what transposition is wanted.

"Stet" means to disregard a copyreading change; that is, literally, copy it *"the way it stood."*

AID TO LEGIBILITY—It is useful for copyists, and for some copypreparers with scrawly handwriting, to be aware of a technique for helping avoid a misreading of *n*'s for *u*'s and *m*'s for *w*'s in longhand-written copy. It is simply that a short line is drawn *above* an *n*, and *under* a *u* . . . a slightly longer one *over* an *m*, *under* a *w*.

BOTTOM-OF-PAGE BREAK—When a story runs more than one page, make the "break" to a succeeding page coincide with a paragraph break (instead of the earlier style of deliberately breaking in midsentence) and put the word "more" in parentheses in the bottom right-hand corner of the page. Note, please, that this is not an inflexible rule; if following it would produce awkward spacing (too much or too little) at the bottom of the page, go ahead and make the break in midsentence.

Index

Index